AS THEY LIKED IT

AS THEY LIKED IT

A Study of Shakespeare's Moral Artistry

ALFRED HARBAGE

UNIVERSITY OF PENNSYLVANIA PRESS
Philadelphia

TO ELIZA

CONTENTS

I

PLEASURABLE EXCITEMENT

II

PLEASURABLE REASSURANCE

Foreword to the Second Edition

Except for an altered subtitle and the correction of typographical errors, this book is reissued without revision. It is my favorite among the books I have written, and still represents truly my view of an important aspect of Shakespeare's art. Perhaps I have mistaken 'simplicity' for the 'simple truth' and critical naïveté for innocence, but I have decided to let the argument stand without cautious modification. Concessions can be made in this brief foreword.

I now wish that there were less opening fanfare in the Preface—too jaunty in its generalizations, too intrusive in tone for an essay rebuking critical intrusiveness. I believe that my study will be more persuasive if the reader will skip the Preface and begin with the first chapter. I regret that the strictures upon modern criticism are confined to the historical school. I have since produced 'historical criticism' somewhat copiously myself, and my intention was not to reject a particular school of critics but only to resist appropriation of Shakespeare by specialists of any kind. The historical critics were the most conspicuous specialists at the time this book was written. They have since been replaced in prominence by the formalist and interpretive critics, and I would feel more happy about my book if it offered more explicitly a token resistance to these. So far as criticism is concerned, although some of my chapters may obscure the fact, my final allegience is to unsystematized appreciation.

Foreword

My idea was, and remains, that Shakespeare is not an artistic moralist but a moral artist, and that the more widely we are willing to share his plays with the 'generality' the more we will find in them to share. The word *They* in my title refers to the original audience, as free delegates of a susceptible and aspiring humanity. It is not intended to suggest the masses in Shakespeare's time or any other. It does not indicate a belief on my part that the greater the number of ready consumers the greater the art. This is a more generous notion than its opposite, but equally fallacious, contradicted by the actual art of all ages including, conspicuously, our own.

We now know more about Elizabethan audiences than we once did, and we know there were more kinds than one. A mass audience existed, but Shakespeare did not write for it. It would not have liked the contemplative, the enigmatic, the reticent elements in his art—the subtleties with which he shaded, and by shading authenticated, the projection of essentially simple ideals. A coterie audience existed, but Shakespeare did not write for that either. The dramatic art it preferred was as flat in its reversed way as the glib art of the masses. Shakespeare's audience was large and heterogeneous, drawn from the general public, but a selective principle was at work. There were other theatres than the Globe, and other writers for the Globe itself. Shakespeare and his audience found each other, in a measure created each other. He was a quality writer for a quality audience. It is difficult to see how we can reach any other conclusion. The great Shakespearean discovery was that quality extended vertically through the social scale, not horizontally at the upper genteel, economic, and academic levels.

The ideals projected to please his audience were neither complex nor original with him—he does not qualify as a moral philosopher—, but those ideals are more apt to seem conventional now than they did then. They appear conventional now partly because Shakespeare espoused them and infused them with such power as to help them to prevail. It is hard to determine to what extent one is being anachronistic in speaking of his 'basic conformity with the most deeply-rooted moral convictions of men.' Deeply-rooted *when?* And with *what* men? To a greater extent than we are aware, Shakespeare and his audience created the humane climate of subsequent generations, including, one hopes, our own. My counting of his good and evil characters is a radical critical method, and more than a little ludicrous. In his own day and earlier, the counting would have seemed less radical than the implication of the totals, and considerably less ludicrous. It had not been the habit of men to look so hopefully at Man.

My foreword threatens to become as aggressive as my Preface. Perhaps it too should be skipped. But such prompting is needless; it is even conceivable that readers will prefer to skip directly to the plays. Shakespeare wrote no forewords, no prefaces, no criticism. He never intruded. He was simply there.

Cambridge, Mass.
August, 1960

PREFACE

Shakespeare is just the poet whom Plato would banish from the ideal republic and Aristotle would attempt to reprieve. No personal animus underlies this contention. If the proscription were sustained and our poet should trudge off to the hinterland, his native wood-notes and fine frenzies forever hushed, one suspects that the sighs of Plato would be deeper than those of the Stagirite. It was all a matter of high philosophical policy. Morality is the stock in trade of a Shakespeare and a Plato alike, but they conduct rival stalls. One can imagine the philosopher looking tolerantly enough at the throngs trading across the way if the poet's wares did not so much resemble his own. The folk must have playthings, and art in itself need not be dangerous. But this particular kind of artist, this poet or fictionist, deals not in enticing arrangements of colors and planes and musical sounds but in *morality*—the qualities and actions of men! It is a bad business, because he deals not as a moralist but as an artist. He is philosophically irresponsible, and he fashions his wares for the world as it is and not as it ought to be.

The Platonic indictment is clearcut and reasonable—more so than the Aristotelian defense. The latter is hard to interpret, but one of its items suggests that poetry has some kind of therapeutic and admonitory function, some kind of utility, aside from its power to please. Aristotle is not himself responsible for the views of all who have joined his party, but during long periods of the history of thought poetry has been defended because of its presumed utility. The poet has been granted citizenship in the republic, with a small dwelling and parcel of land, not in spite of his being an artist dealing with morality, as the Platonists properly allege, but because of his being a moralist in his own right, as the Aristotelians improperly imply. He has escaped banishment on the basis of a legal error. The poets themselves have sometimes fancied themselves in the role of moralist. In a period when the didactic function of poetry was often taken for granted, John Dryden unaggressively endorsed the opposing view that the vocation of the literary artist was only to please, but Thomas Shadwell angrily retorted that he at least refused to be diminished to the stature of a mere fiddler. The writing of plays, the dealing in morality, seems to have gone to Shadwell's head, so that he had come to despise the company of mere artists—fiddlers and their ilk.

The trouble with Shadwell is that he is a moralist without being moral. Shakespeare, in contrast, is moral without being a moralist. It is the purpose of my book to make these remarks seem not quite so cryptic, to add a footnote to the long controversy over the place of the poet in society, and, most ambitiously of all, to say something applicable to play-writing and novel-writing today. The word *poet* is here used in its old sense of *fictionist,* and it is taken for granted that the playwrights and story-tellers of all times must accept Shakespeare as the most successful of their kind. His methods can be analyzed, and, in the particular with which we are here concerned, they can even be imitated. That anything of the kind will result from the influence of the following pages seems, I regret to say, somewhat unlikely. No attempt will be made to refute the charges of Plato. Shakespeare was, we must grant, precisely the poet whom the philosopher had in mind. We must find him guilty, then issue a pardon and let him remain in our midst. Plato drew his illustrations from the really formidable tellers of tales in epic and drama—those who had been loved by countless Athenians through many generations. The Shadwells he might also have wished to expel, but the chances are that he would have considered it scarcely worth the bother.

I must say a word about my materials and methods. I have taken it as a postulate that Shakespeare was a popular artist, one whose work was shaped by the tastes of a large and representative audience, a cross section of the humanity of his day. I have kept such an audience constantly in mind and tried in a measure to be its spokesman. If I seem to have dealt somewhat abruptly with the subject of Elizabethan science and philosophy, the 'frame of reference' with which Shakespearean criticism has lately been so much concerned, it is not through indifference but through conviction that his true 'frame of reference' is less esoteric. Shakespearean criticism in general looms large among my materials. This criticism viewed as a whole provides our safest indication of the nature of the response of Shakespeare's original audience. It is in itself a great human document, and an indispensable check upon the notions of any single critic, including one's own. The need for condensation has often resulted in the selection of a mere phrase or two to suggest some individual's views, and the practice can be very annoying. On those few occasions when I have myself been quoted, I have never felt that the sampling did justice to the rich amplitude of my thought. I have tried, however, to avoid misrepresentation, and although I have indulged occasionally in the luxury of controversy, I have tried to reserve the foreground of my discussion for something more positive. The design of my essay requires that the criticism of the ages in its main bearing be accredited, and I have quarreled only with that small recent portion of it which would establish itself at the expense of all the rest.

I have devoted considerable attention to the sources of Shakespeare's plays but not for the purpose of determining the degree of his indebtedness or lack of indebtedness to particular works. In a larger number of cases than we realize, some lost play may intervene between Shakespeare's and its presumed source, or he may have worked up a fable supplied him orally by one who had seen or heard of the original which we now so zealously study. This fact does not diminish the interest of the extant older versions of his plots. Viewed collectively these older versions present contrasts with Shakespeare's that indicate his tendencies in developing story material and placing emphasis. Although the present study does not treat specifically Shakespeare's habitual attitude toward particular vices and virtues, personal and political, I have gathered the material available, and may use as illustration of the value of source-study the light it throws on his choices in treating sexual transgression. In only six of his thirty-eight

plays is an act of fornication or adultery, as distinct from
the suspicion of such acts, really encompassed; and when
these plays are read in the light of the anterior literature
to which they relate, the fact appears as simply astonishing. Shakespeare was almost as determined an expurgator
as Bowdler. He is practically the only writer who omits
the Jane Shore episode in treating the lives of Edward the
Fourth and Richard the Third, and practically the only
one who refrains from punishing jealous husbands in
comedy by making their wives unfaithful. An author's
moral bias is indicated by what he avoids as well as what
he treats, and the clue to Shakespeare's bias often lies in
the products of other men. Although the fact may not
always be obvious, in the following pages the older works
with which Shakespeare's are compared are viewed mainly
as analogues.

I have treated all thirty-eight plays as truly Shakespeare's except for the first two acts of *Pericles* and the
Fletcherian portions of *King Henry the Eighth* and *The
Two Noble Kinsmen*. The trilogy on the reign of King
Henry the Sixth, I consider not only Shakespearean, but
fascinating plays. That these and others may contain occasional passages composed by some other hand need not
concern us. Whatever Shakespeare allowed to stand in his
text is his by endorsement so far as its content or moral
bearing is concerned. I have paid no attention to the
dramatist's 'periods' or to autobiographical significance in
his plays. There is an unusual hardness about *Troilus and
Cressida*, but there is a hint of such hardness in *Love's
Labour's Lost*. If *The Tempest* is a play of reconciliation,

so also are *A Midsummer Night's Dream* and *As You Like It*. If *King Lear* is pessimistic, as I fail to see, so also is *Romeo and Juliet*. It is highly improbable that *All's Well that Ends Well* and *Measure for Measure* were considered by author or audience as 'bitter' plays. The works which depart most from the Shakespearean norm are *Titus Andronicus* and *Timon of Athens*, the one probably a piece of hasty revision and the other probably an abandoned sketch. What strikes one most forcibly about Shakespeare's plays is their moral homogeneity. He found his way quickly and stayed with it to the end, growing in power and technical skill but changing little in his basic attitudes.

There is always danger in an essay like mine of reasoning from selected evidence, of defending fallacies with excerpts. I can only say that I have been aware of the danger, and have quoted nothing without pondering over the character of the speaker and the context in which the speech occurs. My generalizations, in intention at least, are based on the total content of all the plays; but these plays present a vast and complex realm, and unless one mistakes his memory and judgment to be infallible, he must realize that he writes under correction. My central idea is that Shakespeare's plays are designed to exercise but not to alter our moral notions, to stimulate but not to disturb, to provide at once pleasurable excitement and pleasurable reassurance. Their basic conformity with the most deeply-rooted moral convictions of men is what distinguishes them from the more pretentious fiction of our own day. The latter is often unaware of these convictions or pioneers against them—and as art it pays the penalty. It

excites but does not reassure, disturbs but does not stimulate, engages our interest but does not win our love. Our
minds grope with the apparent necessity of saying yes to its
inversions and negations at the same time that our hearts
say no. To the plays of Shakespeare our hearts say yes,
unmindful of Plato's warning that we are being seduced
into contentment with what is good without being the best.

In my quotations from Shakespeare I have followed
the Kittredge text. My essay has been read in manuscript
by Tucker Brooke of Yale University, Oscar J. Campbell
and Mark Van Doren of Columbia, and Matthias A.
Shaaber and Allan G. Chester of the University of Pennsylvania. I wish to express to them my gratitude for their
generous sacrifice of time, and for their correction and
encouragement. Clerical assistance has been placed at my
disposal by the Committee for the Advancement of Research of the University of Pennsylvania. The index has
been prepared by my wife.

A. H.

Devon, Pennsylvania
June, 1946

PART ONE

Pleasurable Excitement

CHAPTER I

MORAL STIMULUS

People in throngs, of all classes and callings, gathered to see Shakespeare's plays. They came in wherries, on horseback, and on foot, from Cheapside and White Chapel, Westminster and Newington, Clerkenwell and Shoreditch, deserting for an interval their workbenches, their accounts, their studies, their sports, their suits at law, and their suits at court. They preferred the pleasures of the Globe to the pleasures of Brentford and Ware, and if they did not pass coldly by the ale-house doors, at least they reserved enough pennies to pay the gatherers. These people were shorter on the average than we, and the majority were not so well nourished; the women wore voluminous skirts, and most of the men wore high-crowned hats; they had heard some curious rumors about geography and science. In most ways, however, they must have been remarkably like ourselves, for the plays that please us were written to please them. If Shakespeare's plays had reached us by interstellar radio as a specimen of Martian amusements, we would know that the Martians loved language, sometimes melodious, sometimes grand, muscular, and mouth-filling; that they loved stories full of action and adventure; and that they were able to laugh and cry. Above all, we would know that they were creatures of moral sensibility, whose interest could be aroused and held by conflicts of good and evil.

3

What places Shakespeare apart, we often say, is his *poetry*, the loveliness of sounds and images—

> . . . daffodils
> That come before the swallow dares and take
> The winds of March with beauty; violets dim
> But sweeter than the lids of Juno's eyes
> Or Cytherea's breath.[1]

Then we observe a curious thing: that this poetic loveliness —these sounds and images—is always infused with ethical sentiment. Pride and humility are in these flowers, not as opposed but as complementary values: the daffodils are staunch, and the violets worthy to be dowered with the wealth of antique beauty even though they are *dim*. The lines occur after a debate on the respectability of those crossed or, as Perdita says, 'bastard' flowers called gillyvors; and the debate occurs when the mating of a prince and a shepherdess seems impending. It is the prince's father who defends the gillyvor, and thus, unwittingly, any marriage of 'gentler scion to the wildest stock' because all things in nature are natural:

> . . . nature is made better by no mean
> But nature makes that mean.[2]

These are strange associations: the philosophizing king and the shepherdess in her garden; the daffodils, violets, primroses, their very fragrance musically evoked, true flowers all, yet symbols of something more—the reach of nature, the justification of misalliance, the moral standing of the gillyvor or common clove-scented pink! An odd concatenation, but typically Shakespearean.

4

Each lyrical passage has its ethical infusion or its ethical setting. 'Would you have a love song, or a song of good life?' asks Feste in *Twelfth Night*.[3] 'A love song, a love song,' says Sir Toby. 'Ay, ay!' says Sir Andrew. 'I care not for good life.' Then comes the singing of 'O Mistress mine, where are you roaming?' with its

> Journeys end in lovers meeting
> Every wise man's son doth know

and Feste has given them both a love song and a song of good life. George Moore included 'O Mistress mine' in his *Anthology of Pure Poetry*,[4] from which all notes of moral suggestion were to be debarred. Among the sixty-six songs of Shakespeare, Moore found eighteen sufficiently free from taint. Some of the most beautiful, like 'Fear no more the heat o' th' sun' from *Cymbeline*, of course had to be excluded. Rigid consistency would have excluded most of the accepted eighteen. When the question 'Who is Silvia?' is answered, 'Holy, fair, and wise is she,' we are not in an extra-moral atmosphere, nor when the invitation to lie 'Under the greenwood tree' is extended to any 'who doth ambition shun.' Two of the eighteen are charms against molestation, two are laments of the forsaken in love, and four contain jesting allusions to theft, drunkenness, and sexual transgression. Only seven of the songs are actually 'pure'—all of them single stanzas, minuscules of melody like 'Hark, hark! the lark,' 'Where the bee sucks,' and 'Come unto these yellow sands.'

In Shakespeare a little candle shining in the night suggests 'a good deed in a naughty world.'[5] A Tom a Bedlam pieces out his ravings, 'Take heed o' th' foul fiend; obey thy parents; keep thy word justly; swear not; commit not with man's sworn spouse; set not thy sweet heart on proud array. Tom's acold.' [6] A drunkard mutters, 'Well, God's above all, and there be souls must be saved, and there be souls must not be saved.' [7] A clown cadges for money, '. . . but I would not have you to think that my desire of having is the sin of covetousness.' [8] And a Roman cobbler, of all people, puns upon salvation, 'A trade, sir, that I hope I may use with a safe conscience, which is indeed, sir, a mender of bad soles.' [9]

Relevantly or not, in season and out, moral gleams play over the surface and under the surface of Shakespeare's words. Characters like Falstaff and Autolycus constantly debate their moral status. If we begin to wonder what moral effect his service will have upon Falstaff's little page, it is not our priggishness but the playwright's hint that stirs the thought in our minds: 'An you do not make him be hang'd among you, the gallows shall have wrong.' [10] A description of Queen Mab's train leads to a catalogue of human foibles,[11] and moonlight on Belmont suggests fidelity and infidelity in love.[12] The whole of Act Two, Scene Four, of *Twelfth Night* is filled with sweetness, a kind of tender melancholy, and that is its artistic impact, yet the scene places before us a series of curious contradictions on the relative constancy of women and men.[13] Except in a few scenes of *A Midsummer Night's Dream*, there are not thirty consecutive lines in Shakespeare that do not levy upon the vocabulary of ethics, or relate in some way to standards of conduct, to choices between right and wrong.

6

Dr. Johnson was once forced to defend his contention that nothing in Shakespeare matched the description of the temple in Congreve's *Mourning Bride*: 'What I mean is, that you can shew me no passage where there is simply a description of material objects, without any intermixture of moral notions, which produces such an effect.' [14] Here as so often, although not always, Johnson's position was invulnerable. Shakespeare produces his effects, of pleasure or pain, of beauty or ugliness, of tears or laughter, if not by means of, at least to the inevitable accompaniment of, *moral notions*.

The songs have truly no moral intention, and the cobbler's pun no ethical force. We have been making our way where the going is hardest. The moral gleam that is incidental, inconspicuous, or purely verbal, often giving the impression of inadvertence, merely demonstrates a habit of mind. In most of Shakespeare's lines the moral infusion is evidenced not by fitful gleams but by a constant and powerful glow. And such is what we might expect, as a matter of artistic harmony, and of practical tactics, in the work of a great dramatist. The subject matter of a dramatist is action that is related to welfare. Although human beings are interested in all kinds of action—the thrust of a steam-shovel, the flight of a buzzard, the burst of a roman candle—most human beings, at least those found in theatres, seem to be most interested in action among creatures like themselves, involving alternatives of conduct and their consequences, involving competitive individuals and competitive patterns of behavior. What distinguishes the action of drama from acrobatic display is its consequential nature, and to recognize that a dramatist deals with such action is to recognize that he deals with morality. The greater dramatist will do so more abundantly than the lesser.

One way to gauge the intensity and complexity of the moral content of Shakespeare's plays is to compare them with sources and analogues. Since such comparison will concern us frequently in later pages, the present remarks are intended only as suggestive. A source play or story serves Shakespeare as a painter's cartoon. He retains the outline but gives it content, and this content, aside from the glowing colors of his rhetoric, is chiefly moral complexity. What strikes one first about the old play of *King Leir* is the relative blamelessness of its protagonist:

> . . . he, the myrrour of mild patience,
> Puts vp all wrongs, and never gives reply.[15]

Humble and good to begin with, he need not be beaten into humility and goodness; we do not watch fascinated these qualities being forged on the anvil. Cruelly treated by Gonorill, this gentle old man 'put vp well ynough, and seemed not to see the things he saw,' [16] thus preventing us even for one guilty moment from sympathizing with the wicked side. There are no Gloucester and Edmund to give terrible extension to a terrible theme. Contrasts as striking are provided by the character of Hamlet compared either with the traditional figure in Saxo Grammaticus and Belleforest or with the heroes of revenge plays as a class; and by the character of Othello compared with the vengeful *Moro* of Cinthio's *Hecatommithi*.

In the nearest surviving analogue to *The Merchant of*

Venice, Fiorentino's *Il Pecorone*, IV, 1, the villainy of the Jew is presented with no mitigation to trouble our spirits. He has received no injury from Ansaldo (Antonio), but is only a bloody usurer maliciously intent upon the death of a prospering Christian. It is Shakespeare who lets us glimpse Antonio for a moment through Shylock's eyes as the 'fawning publican,' who lets us see him ready, in the future as in the past, to spit upon the man from whom he would borrow, and challenge him, while it still seems safe to do so, to lend as an enemy, and as an enemy to 'exact the penalty.' [17] It is Shakespeare who gives us Shylock's racial pride, his family sentiment, his sense of wounded dignity, his eloquence in pleading his common humanity.[18] And finally it is Shakespeare who gives the Jew arguments more powerful than any to be found in Silvayn's *The Orator* or any analogous work:

> You have among you many a purchas'd slave,
> Which, like your asses and your dogs and mules,
> You use in abject and in slavish parts,
> Because you bought them. Shall I say to you,
> 'Let them be free, marry them to your heirs!
> Why sweat they under burthens? Let their beds
> Be made as soft as yours, and let their palates
> Be season'd with such viands'? You will answer,
> 'The slaves are ours.' So do I answer you.
> The pound of flesh which I demand of him
> Is dearly bought, 'tis mine, and I will have it.[19]

Professor Stoll describes this speech as defending Shylock's claim 'as a right by the analogy of holding slaves.' [20] The claim, however, is *not* defended as a right but is equated with universal wrong. Stoll's description would more nearly fit the words of Silvayn's Jew, who mentions the inhumanities among Christians as things 'which because they are in use seeme nothing terrible at all' [21] and does indeed thus try to palliate his offense. Shylock, instead, is carrying the attack to the enemy, invoking the categorical imperative, suggesting all the unchristian implications in the very words *ours* and *mine*. The change in emphasis is a subtle one, but the result is one of those speeches which are incandescent with moral meaning. There is no need to consider Shylock primarily an object of sympathy or the hero of the play; but he himself, considered in isolation, servile and arrogant, frugal and reckless, affectionate and cruel, is an object of contemplation more provocative than anything to be found elsewhere in the line of pound of flesh stories. For the diverse ways in which he has excited the moral sensibilities of different ages, and no doubt of different individuals in the Elizabethan age itself, Shakespeare and not the vagaries of critics must be deemed responsible.

In the older plays on King John we do not hear, as in Shakespeare, an English monarch, in words filled with shame and reluctance,[22] order the murder of a child; and we do not hear his enemies, one of them a Cardinal, in words equally filled with detestation for murder express the hope that the crime will occur because of the advantages to themselves. These are moralistic murderers all. In Holinshed, Prince Hal prematurely takes the crown from his father on his death bed, and the following colloquy ensues:

in the vein of a moral philosopher, until at last the characters decide to 'step out of these dreary dumps,' [32] gossip
a little, and make plans for a day of stag-hunting. In a
word the incongruity of matter and manner is absolute.
Later in the play, actions so horrible as to render imagination inoperative, to swallow up reflection, ethical or otherwise, and to be viewed only with blank, instinctive repug-
nance, are nevertheless brushed up with Shakespeare's
ethical and imaginative colors. Our reverence for the
dramatist cannot blind us to the monstrousness of the
effect. We are reminded of Seneca's *Phaedra* with Theseus
talking away while piecing together the minced body of
Hippolytus in the fashion of a jigsaw puzzle; yet this particular kind of Senecanism, quite different from anything
to be found in *King Richard the Third* or those earlier but
frequently excellent plays of the Henry VI trilogy, seems
the result of accident rather than conscious intent. It
demonstrates once more that, to Shakespeare, working on
a play however mechanically meant injecting into it 'moral
notions.'

CHAPTER II

MORAL RESPONSE

Dust has long since closed the eyes of the first arrivals, but Shakespeare's audience is living still; there have always been more than enough newcomers to fill the vacant places. The audience has become more vocal with the years, and thousands of books now exist to attest the nature of its response. One thinks of the fierce disputes over the hesitations of Hamlet, the injustice to Shylock, the rejection of Falstaff, the improprieties of Helena, the just deserts of Angelo, the defects of Brutus, the redeeming qualities of Richard II, and the like. It is unreasonable to attribute these disputes to mere eccentricity in critics. They are the inevitable consequence of an aroused interest. They mean that the plays, purposely laden with moral stimulus, have achieved their purpose of inducing moral excitement.

Discussion of 'characters' is the natural product of moral excitement—the token, in fact, of a play's success. The plays contain *foci* of moral interest called 'Hamlet,' 'Falstaff,' 'Lear,' and so on. That this is no fanciful way of describing 'characters' may be readily demonstrated. In actual life the thing we call *character* is a badge pinned upon someone in consequence of the semijudicial operations of the mind of someone else. In a specific case it is that which in one person is perceptible and important to another. A person has as many characters as he has human contacts, and may have a fine one in respect to his friend and a vile one in respect to his enemy. When a sufficient number of persons agree about an individual, they have for practical purposes established *the* character of that individual, but we must recognize that such agreement can be reached only about a few rudimentary and obviously utilitarian traits in any given case. It is such *character*, an oversimplified moral abstraction even in actual life, that a dramatist imitates when he produces a 'character.' He cannot successfully imitate whole persons. The very words involve a contradiction in terms, and an assumption that out of the inkwell can emerge living men with souls. He cannot even imitate, except in almost negligible degree, that aspect of a person which a painter imitates. The painter is limited in the opposite respect. Aristotle evidently believed that there *was* an 'art to find the mind's construction in the face' because he commends Polygnotus as a better painter of character than Zeuxis, but when it came to drama he was well enough content if the makers could show the agents of the action to have moral habits, inclinations and disinclinations. The translators of the *Poetics* must use the words *character* and *manners* almost interchangeably to convey the philosopher's meaning.

Those who deplore 'character-mongering' and condemn the nineteenth century critics for confusing *dramatis personae* with real people are meting out something less than justice. It is easy enough to discern, in 'romantic' as in 'historical' criticism, that those under discussion are not real people but characters in a play. The typical discussion of a Shakespearean character is a tabulation of moral traits, a cry for justice, a plea for tolerance, a query on the nature of good and evil, or an analysis of an ethical dilemma. It is a *sentence*—or else it is an accolade. Imogen is 'an immortal godhead of women.' [1] Cleopatra is 'an intelligent, passionate, astute, heartless, essentially vulgar, and profoundly immoral creature.' [2] Lucio 'has a taste for scandal, but it is a mere luxury of idleness; though his tongue is loose, his heart is simply affectionate, and he is eager to help his friend.' [3] Hamlet's 'whole entanglement with the Ghost, and with the crude morality of vengeance which the plot imposes upon him, fails to bring his own soul to a right utterance, and this stifling of his better potential mind is no small part of his tragedy.' [4] Falstaff is 'a knave without malice, a lyar without deceit; and a knight, a gentleman, and a soldier, without either dignity, decency, or honour.' [5] And, lest the present critic seem to claim exemption, Shylock a few pages back appeared as 'servile and arrogant, frugal and reckless, affectionate and cruel.' [6]

One might go on indefinitely. No group of critics could be more unlike in temperament than those just quoted. They belong to different generations and different schools of criticism, but they speak in similar vein. There is about their remarks, besides the moral emphasis, a quality of abstraction, a freedom from uncertainty, and a disinterestedness easily distinguishable from the mode in which human beings discuss other human beings. An actual person occupies space in our world, and we are a little embarrassed in his presence. We speak of him tentatively, self-consciously. But of the thousands who have told what they think about Hamlet, not one has shown any concern over what Hamlet might think about him. A note of malice, or deference, or hope, or fear enters into our discourse on actual people. The reader may wish to make an experiment. George Santayana in his recent autobiographical writings speaks of old friends and acquaintances with unusual detachment; yet if one will read the chapter on Russell in *The Middle Span* and compare it with the chapter on Hamlet in *Interpretations of Religion and Poetry*, he will observe a wonderful difference. It mattered little to Santayana that Hamlet was a prince, but it mattered greatly that Russell was a lord. In literature a prince is an object of moral contemplation, but in life a lord is a lord.

That our response to Shakespeare's characters is moral is demonstrated in the way we take sides. Why is our attitude toward Polonius contemptuous? It cannot be his folly and conceit because in characters like Bottom and Dogberry these qualities are endearing. Polonius lacks the truly alienating traits of a Thurio or an Aguecheek: he is not cowardly and ungenerous, and his intentions are good. No other father in Shakespeare has so obedient a daughter or so devoted a son. To Claudius he is a trusted counsellor and to Reynaldo a respected master. Polonius nevertheless, we say ill-humoredly, is a pretentious ass. In *The Tempest* there is another counsellor, Gonzalo, who is old, sententious, and something of a bore. To Sebastian and Antonio he appears precisely as Polonius appears to Hamlet. Yet we do not share their view. The reason is not that Gonzalo is a loyal man, because so also is Polonius. Gonzalo indeed is morally the more defective of the two because he knows, as Polonius does not, that the master he faithfully serves has connived at the theft of a diadem. The truth of the matter is that the virtue of Gonzalo is partly composed of the villainy of Sebastian and Antonio. We cannot disdain the one whom these villains disdain. And we cannot love the one whom Claudius trusts and Hamlet despises. Hamlet represents to us the higher morality, and his Polonius becomes our Polonius, whose folly and conceit are only wryly amusing. The folly and conceit of Bottom and Dogberry would cease to be ingratiating if these characters were the agents, even the unwitting agents, of falsehood and wickedenss. Our conception of character in the drama is largely a matter of moral partisanship.

Of course physical traits as well as moral habits and moral affiliations are sometimes written into a character, but such traits are few and rudimentary. Characters are old, young, fat, thin, tall, short, fair or ill-favored. Nearly always the physical trait is also a moral symbol—in extreme cases a stigma like Richard the Third's hump. Falstaff is endowed with as many purely material features as any character in Shakespeare, but observe their effect: The dramatist 'has associated levity and debauch with age, corpulence and inactivity with courage, and has roguishly coupled the gout with military honours, and a pension with the pox.' [7] The unimportance of the material supplement to the immaterial conception is demonstrated when the play is acted. The effect of merging the conception of the dramatist with the body and voice of a living actor is further simplification. Characters have actually fewer dimensions on the stage than in the reader's imagination. Polonius, Gonzalo, and, we might add, York of *Richard the Second* all become futile and somewhat ridiculous old men, none too distinguishable from Justice Shallow. Thin shanks, a white beard, a palsied hand, and a cracked voice are remarkable equalizers.

The definition of Shakespeare's characters as *foci* of a quickened moral interest does not imply that these characters lack reality for reader or spectator. They are *real* enough, in the moral world, more real than actual people. It is natural that members of the audience should write about their childhood or muse about their doings offstage. We must note, however, that these characters never leave the stage to take their repose or order their dinner, but to make amends, perpetrate further misdeeds, or to shuffle off moral inconsistencies before private audiences—to reveal their *true selves*. They are vouchsafed no ethical rest periods. Amusing though it may be to observe how the plays constantly trick us into giving ourselves away, into taking sides and sending Shakespeare's 'airy nothings' off to heaven or to hell, there is no reason why we should feel guilty about the matter. It is the twentieth-century condemnation of the tendency to view the characters as *real*, which, to repeat, is the natural response and the indication of the play's success, that must now be examined. We here enter the realm of controversy, but to salvage rather than to destroy—to plead for the authority of Shakespearean criticism as a whole, against that present-day portion of it that would nullify all the rest.

Fortunately we hear little any more about Art for Art's

Sake. In last analysis it was an exclusive movement, calculated to wrest art away from the ordinary man and to
make it the property solely of the virtuoso. It was really
a movement toward art for the critic's sake, or for the
aesthete's sake; and the responses of people generally,
morally colored as such responses are bound to be, were
made to appear laughably inept. The prevailing fashion in
Shakespearean criticism has an analogous tendency to wrest
the plays away from the ordinary reader. This 'historical'
or 'objective' criticism has produced no slogan, but sincerely purports to work for honesty's sake or for the truth's
sake, unaware of the hazard of its becoming a movement
toward art for the scholar's sake. When an older critic is
detected speaking of Hamlet or Falstaff or Shylock as a
contemporary of his own, and evaluating conduct in terms
of his own moral code and observation of life instead of in
terms of Elizabethan dramatic technique, science, and
philosophy, he is accused of confusing art and reality, of
being ignorantly misleading, anachronistic, hopelessly romantic. Yet the very term 'romantic criticism' is a mis-
nomer. It is a mistake to suppose that the impulse to view
the characters as *real*, and to evaluate them subjectively
in the light of moral experience, came with the Romantic
Movement and the writings of Morgann, Goethe, Schlegel, and Coleridge. When Pope says 'every single character in Shakespeare is as much an individual, as those in life
itself,' [8] or Theobald exclaims on 'the mastery of his
portraits' [9] or Dr. Warburton on 'the amazing sagacity
with which he investigates every hidden spring and wheel
of human action,' [10] or when all the others repeat the

cliché that Shakespeare's characters are rather nature itself than copies of nature, we have an indication of illusions in these early readers similar in kind if not in completeness to the illusions in readers like Coleridge. It has been pointed out [11] that treating the characters as actual persons was merely the practical turn finally given to the attitude underlying the cliché. Had the eighteenth century critics been compelled to abandon their judicial and generalizing habit, had they been compelled to defend or illustrate their cliché, they could have done so only by 'character-mongering.' The results, to be sure, would not have been the same as those produced by other critics and other ages, and might have seemed at times highly formalized. John Dennis, an admirable critic in many ways, wrote in 1711 that 'Never was any Buffoon eloquent, or wise, or witty, or virtuous. All the good and ill Qualities of a Buffoon are summ'd up in one Word, and that is a Buffoon.' [12] He is speaking of Menenius, but his words make us reflect upon Falstaff. Even the foes of Falstaff concede that he is at least 'eloquent' and 'witty,' and Dennis would have had to view these qualities not as character traits in Falstaff but as literary indiscretions in Shakespeare. We notice, however, a reluctance on the part of Dennis's contemporaries to accept him as their spokesman. The conventions which had been imposed upon the age, resulting for instance in the perpetual banishment of the Fool from stage performances of *King Lear,* and the expulsion of all qualities except comic ferocity from stage renderings of Shylock, must be viewed with double skepticism. These conventions have no authority so far as Elizabethan attitudes are concerned.

An age nearer the Elizabethan in point of time need not have been nearer it in point of spirit, and the Elizabethans who could tolerate Lear with Fool may have been able to tolerate Shylock with pathos. But more to the point in the present connection is the fact that in the eighteenth century many before Morgann were dissatisfied with stage interpretations of Shakespeare's characters. In the glosses and *obiter dicta* of the early editors, Theobald, Warburton, Johnson, there is often a species of refinement prophetic of so-called 'romantic' criticism. As far back as there is any record, the audience was thinking of the characters as 'real' and was passing moral judgments upon their conduct.

The Shakespearean criticism of Elmer E. Stoll is so distinguished that it cannot be mentioned except with deference, but the reiterated text, 'It is poetically, dramatically, not psychologically, that the characters are meant to interest us,' [13] seems so self-evident if it implies only a distinction between art and science that one wonders why it should need to have been expounded with such strenuous persistence. It is certainly true that psychological responses, accurate in detail, are not available to a playwright. He may not let his characters lapse into sullen silence or become too incoherent in their wrath; they must keep talking, must even be intelligibly insane. Miranda must be emotionally experienced on the day, so to speak, of her emotional birth, and Juliet must be a passionate woman although only fourteen 'come Lammas Eve.' [14] We are not supposed to ponder whether she would be sexually 'awakened'—or whether Othello has an inferior brain because he accepts the particular evidence provided by Iago. In the latter case, the question is only whether a husband can be induced to believe in the guilt of an innocent wife; and the answer is that of course he can, that no one is proof against a plot. In art we take the symbol for the fact. The attention devoted to Iago's methods, the display of intrigue, is a littleness in the play. These methods are just practicable enough to arouse our skepticism, distracting our minds from a more profound interest—as if whole acts had been devoted to the *method* by which Macbeth murdered Duncan. Yet in the play either as it is or as it might have been, the scientific likelihood of Othello's credulity is not the point at issue. On the few occasions when Shakespeare launches into scientific psychology, a matter of clinical demonstration, we have the few occasions when he appears naïf. The good Duke Humphrey's exposure of the 'miracle' of Saunder Simpcox, on the principle that sight suddenly given a man born blind would enable him to 'distinguish of colors' but not 'nominate them all,' [15] is exhibited as a marvel of astuteness; Shakespeare almost sounds trumpets in our ears. It does not follow, of course, that because he was not a modern scientist the playwright was not a keen observer. Trinculo released from his fear of Caliban becomes very contemptuous of the monster, in the way of a small boy.[16] It is a natural touch, and Shakespeare is full of such touches. His observation often goes deep. Sigmund Freud has analyzed the character of King Richard the Third and explained the 'hidden' motives of his conduct, evidently unaware that the very motives deduced are explicitly stated by the character in an earlier Shakespearean play.[17] The fact remains, however, that the truth in Shakespeare's characterization is not of a scientific kind, and the detection of fallacies is the easiest of exercises.

What we need to determine is the implications of the statement, 'It is poetically, dramatically, not psychologically, that the characters are meant to interest us.' *Poetically, dramatically, psychologically*—what do these words really mean? Which of them describes our interest in the motives and value of behavior, our interest in morality? If the word *morally* were to be substituted for one of them, it would have to be the last, and if we said 'It is poetically, dramatically, not morally that the characters are meant to interest us,' we would be ignoring the connotation of the word *characters* itself, as well as the testimony of every age and nearly every individual who has left a record of the nature of this interest. It is true that the characterization is poetic and dramatic rather than scientific, but it is not true that the characterization is poetic and dramatic rather than something else which the word *psychologically* imperfectly describes and partially obscures; we are distracted by unconscious quibbling. Whether natural or not, the characters are symbolic of what is natural. We fill in the outlines and reconcile the inconsistencies with such materials as are at our disposal. These characters are the containers into which we pour the varying ingredients of our own natures, the ciphers we decode with our own keys, the clay we mould in our own images.

William Butler Yeats was himself a poet and playwright, and presumably as likely as anyone to escape moral preoccupations in reading literature, but he responds to Shakespeare like all the rest of us. After a polemic against the utilitarians who have decried the character of Richard the Second, Yeats turns upon Henry the Fifth, who proves to be a man 'remorseless and undistinguished,' a man of 'gross vices' and 'coarse nerves' speaking a 'resounding rhetoric.' [18] What Yeats gives us is not, as he supposes, a protest against the hounding down of sin, but merely a new sinner. He effects a transfer, and places Richard with the lambs and Henry with the goats. He is interested in two characters, which for him have become two men. In view of his judgments upon the nature and value of these men, we cannot say that he is chiefly interested *poetically* and *dramatically* as these words are commonly used. The nineteenth-century Shylock could be reconstructed out of the shards of Stoll's twentieth-century Shylock, who is 'given his due—a full chance to speak up and make a fair showing for himself,' [19] who has, 'to an extraordinary degree, the proportions and lineaments of humanity and of his race,' [20] who is 'given now and then a touch of almost incompatible tenderness.' [21] No susceptible reader, however determined, can refrain from speaking of Shakespearean characters as 'real' and passing moral judgments upon them. On one occasion Professor Stoll tells us that Falstaff's 'catechism on the battlefield and his deliverances on honour are to be taken as coming not from his heart of hearts but out of his wits to cover his shame.' [22] For Professor Stoll, in unguarded moments, a character has 'a heart of hearts' just as for Mrs. Jameson.

Among the critics accused of being romantic, subjective,

anachronistic, Coleridge figures as the leading culprit. In the lecture series of 1811–12, he made what is probably the most famous single pronouncement on a Shakespearean character:

Shakespeare wished to impress upon us the truth, that action is the chief end of existence—that no faculties of intellect, however brilliant, can be considered valuable, or indeed otherwise than as misfortunes, if they withdraw us from, or render us repugnant to action, and lead us to think and think of doing, until the time has elapsed when we can do anything effectively . . . [Hamlet] is a man living in meditation, called upon to act by every motive human and divine, but the great object of his life is defeated by continually resolving to do, yet doing nothing but resolve.

Acquaintances of Coleridge were among his audience. 'This is a satire on himself,' said one of them to H. C. Robinson. 'No,' replied Robinson, 'it is an elegy.' [23] That Coleridge's Hamlet was created in his own image is not a twentieth-century discovery. A crime has not been *detected*, but created by retroactive legislation. Of what does the crime consist? It would be absurd to say that Coleridge was unqualified to read the plays, or that he should not have let them mean to him what they did. His only indictable offense was in speaking out. He not only expressed his views but assumed them to be correct—a defect in manners. In commenting on a quite sensible gloss by old Theobald on Caesar's remark that Cassius 'hears no music,' Coleridge exclaimed (although not publicly), 'O Theobald! . . . The meaning was here too deep for a line tenfold the length of thine to fathom!' [24] The words 'he hears no music' would have thrown a reader of Coleridge's sensibilities into an ague of response, and made him pay out tenfold the length of line necessary. Perhaps there is justice in his being reproved now as he reproved Theobald then. Time takes its revenges. Nevertheless we must grant that, in speaking out, Coleridge was only doing what all critics must, and that in trusting so implicitly in his own judgments he was guilty only of a defect in manners from which the rest of us are by no means free. His more grave offense was one that most of us are in little danger of committing: it was having his views so generally accepted. The terrible thing about Coleridge's criticism—like Bradley's—is its tremendous success.

Perhaps the range of acceptance is the test of great criticism as of great art, such criticism bringing us discovery that is also recognition, a sense that this particular observor has seen something the rest of us were about to see. Yet the ultimate effect of a Coleridge or a Bradley is to narrow our horizons. Our imagination becomes less free after reading him, and his Hamlet tends to become ours. With Professor Stoll's protest that Shakespeare 'now is Dowden, Swinburne, Bradley, Raleigh, indeed, no longer himself,'[25] we can feel much sympathy, but in place of that word *himself* we had better substitute *ourself*, lest some new critic intervene. The substitution, to be sure, may be not quite in line with the 'historical' critic's intention. Whatever the intention, the influence of the 'historical' school of criticism has been emancipating. Arguments that Hamlet is a man of action, Shylock a comic villain, Falstaff a mere buffoon, or, as Schücking proposes, that those signs of remorse we seemed to see in Macbeth are only indications that he is a very nervous fellow,[26] are valuable as counter-propaganda. They restore a balance and let us read Shakespeare subjectively once more, as he should be read, released from the subjectivities of the more persuasive critics without being bound anew by these less persuasive ones. Schücking's ukase, in attempting to stem 'the subjective current in the contemplation of Shakespeare,'[27] to the effect that 'Little good can result from even the most sagacious verdict of the mere amateur,'[28] need not make us withhold our verdicts, or dismiss completely those of Johnson, Coleridge, Bradley and the rest, who brought to the plays only an interest in, and imperfect knowledge of, humanity instead of expertness in dramatic technique. Professor Stoll uses the fatal analogy that reading a play should be like reading musical score, evidently forgetting that musical score is subtended by the exact science of mathematics. Morgann, he says in objecting to Morgann's Falstaff, 'cannot read score,'[29] but no two readers or spectators of the role of Falstaff have any exact science to which to refer—nothing, indeed, but their own infinitely variable human natures. When Professor Stoll says that the merry rogues of Shakespeare such as Autolycus 'leave us today somewhat cold,'[30] we are reminded inevitably of Dowden's yearning 'to be off for once on an adventure of roving and rogueing with Autolycus.'[31] What we have here is a contrast of temperament, either between two individuals or, if Stoll is speaking authoritatively for 'us today,' between two generations. Only a policeman could regulate these differences in temperament. Yeats, as we have seen, was attracted by Richard

II, and so in more qualified fashion was Walter Pater,[32] but Swinburne, unlike these two or Coleridge, considered Richard a womanish rascal,[33] thus demonstrating that not all poets are enamored of Richard's poetic gift. Sir Edmund Chambers, whose criticism, incidentally, is highly subjective and therefore presumably amateur, sees Vincentio in *Measure for Measure* as indulging in 'the antics of a cat with a mouse'[34] and not at all as a symbol of Providence as so many others have done. For Quiller-Couch, Isabella was a 'base procuress,' but for Professor Sisson she represents something in womanhood which Shakespeare 'reveres with all his heart.'[35] And thus it goes. Nothing is more easy—or more vain—than this pitting of critics against each other. All that the conflicts prove is that we respond to Shakespeare morally, and therefore earnestly and in diverse ways.

There is actually no such thing as 'historical' or 'objective' criticism—except possibly in matters of prosody and the like. With the first step into the realm of larger meanings, the subjective element enters in. We need only compare the opinions of two different 'historical' critics for *prima facie* evidence of this truth. It is a matter of *emphasis*, proclaims one of them; but emphasis, like beauty, seems to dwell in the eye of the beholder. Othello looked less black to Desdemona than to Brabantio, and more credulous to me than to my fellow playgoer. Then comes the disgusted comment, 'a work of art means anything, everything—that is, nothing,—and what is the use of discussing it?'[36] No use whatever if the object of that discussion is to carry a motion by unanimous vote, or to establish a fact as a physicist establishes a formula. It cannot be done. But there is a danger of overstating the evil consequences of our failure. Although it is true that disputes over characters and their motives derive from the conflicting moral interests and predilections of the disputants, and sometimes it seems that we are being told how Shakespeare should have interpreted the play if the critic had written it, it does not follow that either play or critique is meaningless. The play, of course, has meaning and even *a* meaning. *Hamlet* the play means that sin has sorrowful consequences, and the behavior of Hamlet the prince means that he is a better man than Claudius. A critic may legitimately see defects in Hamlet and merits in Claudius, but if he concludes that Claudius is a better man than Hamlet, or, in view of the indiscriminate way in which wages are paid, that one might just as well sin as do otherwise, he has mistaken the meaning of the play. There are limits within which sane criticism must reside. More likely to exceed these limits than the criticism of 'character-mongering' is that hyper-aesthetic kind which ignores the content of the play almost entirely, and resembles 'program notes' on a symphony. In general, the limits are broad enough to give hospitality to many interpretations, articulate and inarticulate, varying in detail in the degree that sane minds and moral natures vary in their exact configuration. It is as mistaken to conceive of an Elizabethan audience containing no Coleridges as to conceive of one composed wholly of Coleridges. The pathos of Shylock, the inertia of Hamlet, the genius of Falstaff, may seem more emphatic to later ages than to the Elizabethan; however, they are not created by these later ages but are in the plays to begin with. It is of the nature of art that it be variously received, and of great art that it mean many things to many men. All criticism that has had a respectful hearing resides safely within the limits of Shakespeare's meaning. Some critics seem to have more representative responses than others and are more readily accepted as spokesmen by the inarticulate, and some critics have more persuasive styles and better manners than others. We must always suspect that the one campaigning for *a* meaning in Shakespeare narrow enough to put others in the wrong is inordinately devoted to *his* meaning. But this, too, is excusable. Only a seer can deduce Shakespeare's *intention* unless that intention be defined as providing stimulus in order to get a response. Quite obviously, however, Shakespeare did not consider the insane and amoral members of his potential audience numerous enough to make appeal to their natures a rewarding endeavor.

An interesting variety of 'historical' criticism is that which attempts to expound Shakespeare, not in terms of Elizabethan dramatic technique and character types in the manner of Stoll and Schücking, but in terms of Elizabethan science and philosophy. One way to adjudicate the differences of opinion among critics, to reduce apparent confusion, seems to be to establish the 'frame of reference' —to discover what the plays meant to their original audience as a separate identity. Renaissance cosmology, statecraft, physiology and psychology or 'the doctrine of humors,' superstition, Machiavellian *virtu*, and the like are investigated in books and articles, occasionally somewhat myopic but often interesting and useful. These works add to our store of information, aid in the explication of obscure passages, and enable us to read with new understanding, if not the plays of Shakespeare with which they are concerned, at least the plays of writers like Chapman with which they are not concerned. A work of this type is nearly always divided into two parts. Part One is a learned, educational, and even entertaining survey of some branch of Elizabethan learning, often revealing to the thoughtful the constancy of man's ideas about his universe, and the fact that a great deal of common sense may lurk behind quaint terminology. It is when we turn to Part Two, in which the plays of Shakespeare are enclosed in the frame of reference provided in Part One, that we encounter a difficulty. The plays prove as nimble in slipping out of the Elizabethan frame as out of any other, and can be kept within it only by acts of minor violence committed by the investigator. There is always an imperfect correspondence, a hiatus, between the play and the scholar's explication. An illustration may be offered from one of the best books of the type, Professor Lily B. Campbell's *Shakespeare's Tragic Heroes, Slaves of Passion*. In one chapter of this work, *Hamlet* is analyzed as a tragedy of grief on the principle that it, like the other tragedies, is patterned 'upon the edicts of the philosophers in their anatomies of the passions,' [37] and three grieving sons are brought to our attention—Hamlet, who is apathetic, Laertes, who is violent, and Fortinbras, who is equable. In a word, the schematization of the philosophers, with their three effects of grief, is read into the play, at the expense of bringing forth

34

Fortinbras, whom we had never thought of as such, in the role of a grieving son. Truly enough Shakespeare seems to have been aware of the theoretical advantages of striking a nice balance between apathy and violence in grief, and we must thank Professor Campbell for instructing us in this fact, but when Claudius advises Hamlet on the proper way to grieve—

> With one auspicious and one dropping eye,
> With mirth in funeral and with dirge in marriage,
> In equal scale weighing delight and dole,—[38]

he strikes us as having become infected by too much conversation with Polonius. Even though Shakespeare may not be mocking, as one suspects, the over-simplification of the moral philosophers with that 'one auspicious and one dropping eye,' he is certainly not presenting Hamlet as a slave of passion because of his inability to pattern his conduct upon Claudius's easy recipe.

Two major flaws appear in this learned approach to the plays. One is that fiction does not conform in detail to the philosophy of its age; fictional characters in our own day are not conceived by authors or interpreted by readers in terms of basal metabolism and the activities of the ductless glands in spite of all we now know about these subjects. The second flaw is more grave. It does not follow because resemblances appear in a philosophical system and a play that the play is 'patterned' on the system. The system may not be a cause but a parallel effect. When our children say that the sun is falling behind the barn, they are expressing no stubborn allegiance to the Ptolemaic system but describing what the sun actually seems to do. The ultimate frame of reference of Renaissance moral philosopher as of Renaissance playwright was the visible phenomena of the world, and both philosopher and playwright saw sanguine, phlegmatic, choleric, and melancholy men, just as we still see cheerful, dull, irritable and gloomy men, or, in the words of the vulgar, 'good fellows, dopes, crabs,' and 'wet-blankets.' Hamlet appears to be a gloomy man who under other circumstances might be cheerful enough, and to say that he is a 'victim of melancholy adust as it is derived from the sanguine humor,'[39] is to transpose terms but not elucidate the text. When Professor Lawrence counters the statement of Quiller-Couch that Isabella is 'a base procuress . . . mating a pair without wedlock' by explaining 'the binding force of the Elizabethan betrothal' which 'confers marital rights,'[40] we seem to witness a triumph of the learned critical approach—until we reflect that people generally have never thought of Isabella as a 'procuress' in the first place. What requires explication in this instance is not the play but the temperament of Quiller-Couch. The instincts of the average person are reliable enough in such matters. It is true that Isabella's protégée forces herself on a man who does not want her, as Helena also does, but it is ultra-refinement to view their acts as a species of rape and to place Mariana and Helena in a class with Arabella of Hardy's *Jude the Obscure*. Average instincts again are a reliable guide. Mariana and Helena are not snaring men too good for them, and are therefore neither prurient nor base; their acts are instinctively evaluated as a means to an end, and the end is

36

no different from that of women generally. There is no question that research into contemporary customs and conceptions is valuable, if only as a service to those who have lost the habit of viewing life simply and directly; but, without making any plea for ignorance, we may express the comforting opinion that Shakespeare's language is sufficiently untechnical and his patterns of behavior sufficiently unformalized for a quite unhistorical frame of reference —human nature as it still appears—to serve most readers adequately. Knowledge of Shakespeare's times is, of course, a gain; but if stress upon the importance of such knowledge leads the individual reader to distrust his own responses, the gain will be obliterated by a devastating loss. The plays themselves will appear to have become mere history.

The danger, however, seems not very imminent. The merit of a treatise like Professor Campbell's, aside from its valuable presentation of facts, lies in the author's ability to depart from her thesis and indulge in some vehement non-historical criticism:

And though God's vengeance is slow, there is no doubt in the mind of any reader of *Hamlet* that the King has suffered punishment from the moment when he committed his crime,—in the fear and suspicion and unrest of his days, in the increasing battalions of his troubles, in the sick soul which could not rid itself of passion or the fruits of passion to find peace with God. Nor can any reader doubt that the eternal vengeance of God is to fall upon the King.[41]

It is difficult to perceive what frame of reference the critic is here using other than her own essentially religious and moral nature. Even though Shakespeare had failed to give a cue with 'flights of angels' singing the sweet Prince to his rest (as he fails in *Lear*), the critic could have been relied upon to supply a heaven for Hamlet and a hell for Claudius. We may demur at the sentence of 'eternal vengeance' or even point out that the catalogue of the King's sufferings prior to death serves equally well for the Prince's, but we can only admire the critic's whole-hearted partisanship in her treatment of her 'slaves of passion.' And, to reiterate—here as always, moral stimulus has evoked a moral response.

The questionable assumptions of contemporary criticism have been dwelled upon thus long in a spirit of defense, not attack. The great body of Shakespearean criticism as a whole is a valuable and illuminating product of our culture. It should not in any part be dismissed in a tone of annoyance or contempt. Pre-romantic, romantic, post-romantic—nearly all of it is good in its kind. The critics speak a common language and testify collectively if not individually to the nature of the plays and the nature of human responses. A simple illustration will sum up the general bearing of this testimony. Elmer E. Stoll and George L. Kittredge must be accepted without hesitation as mature, intelligent, distinguished students of Shakespeare, equally conversant with his text and with the literature of his day. Stoll considers Falstaff a coward, but Kittredge, even with the advantage of access to Stoll's argument, considers Falstaff a courageous man.[42] Who can arbitrate the conflicts of Titans? All we can say is that the response to Shakespeare is moral, and differs in different men—with one addition, which will be the subject of the following chapter: Although Stoll and Kittredge differ over whether Falstaff is cowardly or courageous, neither of them doubts for a moment that in Shakespeare courage is a good thing and cowardice a bad, and that the bad things always are distinguishable from the good.

CHAPTER III

HIGHROAD LEADING NOWHERE

The earliest critics took Shakespeare's morality for granted. When the subject was opened to debate by Dr. Johnson, a distinction was made that has been observed with remarkable unanimity ever since. It is one of those points, too infrequently noted, upon which outstanding critics of different ages and different schools agree. The distinction may be expressed thus: Shakespeare is moral but not a moralist; if his plays teach at all, they do so casually rather than by conscious design; they are not didactic but exist within a moral frame.

In extracting first the positive element in this pronouncement, we must begin with Johnson's 'From his writings a system of social duty may be selected, for he that thinks reasonably must think morally.' [1] To Goethe, Shakespeare's thinking morally means that he safely relies upon 'his own pure inner nature,' [2] and to Schlegel that he never confounds 'the eternal line of separation between good and evil.' [3] In Coleridge the thought takes its most famous figurative expression. Shakespeare keeps *at all times the high road of life.* [4] Hazlitt says, 'he was a moralist in the same sense in which nature is one,' [5] and Birch indignantly concurs—highly incensed because Shakespeare 'insisted

upon the natural goodness of the human heart' [6] instead of
on the doctrine of original sin. Gervinus takes issue with
Birch's charges of irreligion, but praises the morality of the
plays in much the same terms as Johnson's: Shakespeare's
poetry 'is inseparably interwoven with his ethical feelings,
because he took life as a whole, and was himself a whole
man.' [7] Dowden finds him moral 'like nature and like the
vision of human life itself.' [8] Croce, opposed though he is
to the idea that literature has a moral function, devotes a
whole chapter to Shakespeare's underlying moral 'sentiments,' and calls him a 'pre-philosopher' with predilections bearing 'a strong imprint of Christian ethics.' [9] Professor Stoll is at one here with critics of the nineteenth
century: 'the verities are unshaken, the moral values and
even the social sanctions are unbroken' and we are made
'to feel deeply and rightly, and to think sanely.' [10] So
with John Dover Wilson: 'few men have ever lived pos-
sessing more moral sanity than Shakespeare,' whom 'we
trust as we trust no other writer.' [11] The reader, says Mark
Van Doren, 'will be safe from outrage because he will
always know his bearings.' [12] It is Shakespeare's acceptance
of 'current morality' [13] that George Bernard Shaw attacks,
but another popular lecturer, Robert G. Ingersoll, fer-
vently commends: 'Shakespeare pursued the highway to
the right.' [14] An English and an American scholar have
written on Shakespeare 'normality,' both echoing the Cole-
ridgean phrase: the plays, says C. H. Herford, stick 'to the
broad highway of experience,' [15] and their author, says
Hardin Craig, went 'about as far on the open road as a man
could go.' [16]

The second item in this remarkable display of critical agreement may be suggested to the reader by a reminder of all that has been said about Shakespeare's objectivity or impartiality. Again we begin with Johnson: Shakespeare 'seems to write without any moral purpose . . . ; his precepts and axioms drop casually from him.' [17] Goethe says, he wrote 'without reference to any established religion' [18] and Schlegel, that we perceive in him 'a certain cool indifference.' [19] For reasons that will presently become apparent, Coleridge, although the phrase 'wonderful philosophical impartiality' [20] is his, must be omitted from the present roll-call; but not Hazlitt, with his widely endorsed, 'In one sense [the present sense], Shakespeare was no moralist at all.' [21] And thus it goes—with Dowden's 'Shakespeare provides no answers, he puts the questions greatly'; [22] Croce's 'he is not a poet of particular practical ideals' but of 'undecided conflicts'; [23] Stoll's 'he has no theology or theodicy, no philosophy or "message"'; [24] Wilson's 'he is utterly unlike a school-master or a preacher or a professor'; [25] and so on. It would be pointless to extend the list. No thought is more commonly expressed in the literature on the poet.

This antinomy, widely perceived, that in Shakespeare's plays we have morality but not moralizing, draws different responses from different individuals and explains many apparent contradictions in Shakespearean criticism. Johnson's critical creed required moralizing of a poet, who must 'disregard present laws and opinions, and rise to general and transcendental truths . . . as the interpreter of nature and the legislator of mankind.' [26] The absence of moralizing in Shakespeare must therefore be condemned as a fault:

> . . . he makes no just distribution of good or evil, nor is always careful to show in the virtuous a disapprobation of the wicked; he carries his persons indifferently through right and wrong, and at the close dismisses them without further care, and leaves their examples to operate by chance. This fault the barbarity of his age cannot extenuate; for it is always a writer's duty to make the world better, and justice is a virtue independent on time or place.[27]

Survival of this attitude, less consciously assumed or less frankly owned, explains statements as widely removed from each other as Taine's on Shakespeare's 'fire and immorality,' [28] and Santayana's on his leaving life 'without a setting, and consequently without a meaning.' [29] For Taine the apparent absence of moral channeling in the Shakespearean stream, so different from what could be found in Racine, meant only one thing, and the poet who was not a moralist was 'immoral.' Comparison of Shakespeare with Homer, Aeschylus, Dante, or Milton often contains a note of deprecation; he, unlike them, codifies nothing, expresses clear allegiance to no philosophical or religious system. The 'new humanists' have been greatly exercised about the matter; and the disciples of T. S. Eliot have skirmished with it in varying degrees of earnest confusion. For Birch the system should have been orthodox Christianity, but Santayana would be content 'not with this or that system but some system.' [30]

It is remarkable that Johnson, having recorded his objection, seems to have been so little concerned about it. He could read the plays and even edit them without perturbation of spirit. The morality compensated for the lack of moralizing. Shakespeare's suspended premises so to speak, existing in the absence of conclusions, satisfied Johnson as they have failed to satisfy Shaw or Tolstoy, or, in political and social directions at least, Whitman and many more. Johnson tabled his own motion of censure because, in final analysis, Shakespeare's morality was Johnson's morality.

Shakespeare's morality, his suspended premises, for reasons which will become apparent has been acceptable to most readers. For many, the morality has meant that Shakespeare is a moralist. We are dealing here with habits of thought and habits of language. Just as the absence of moralizing meant to Taine that Shakespeare was immoral, so the presence of morality meant to Coleridge that Shakespeare was a moralist. Coleridge considered the Johnsonian accusation 'cruel,'[31] as well he might. Given the premises, Coleridge was ready enough to supply the conclusions—to put into words the 'lessons' conveyed by a character or situation. So also, sometimes with an alienating dogmatism, have been critics like Ulrici in their search for 'poetical justice,' but the tendency can scarcely be condemned without condemning the Shakespearean method as a whole. The moral stimulus is designed to call forth a moral response, and the absence of explicit statement in the plays invites such a statement from members of the audience. The tendency to extract particular morals or lessons from the plays is so general as to render rebuke of Coleridge's part in it illogical.

There is one phase of the tendency so congenial to our

own day that we are in no position to see it in perspective. It was not Coleridge but Hazlitt, and in a measure Schlegel, who reversed Johnson's sentence upon Shakespeare. For Hazlitt the absence of moralizing was itself a moral virtue:

> . . . for morality (commonly so called) is made up of antipathies; and his talent consisted in sympathy with human nature, in all its shapes, degrees, depressions, and elevations. The object of the pedantic moralist is to find out the bad in everything: his way was to shew that 'there is some soul of goodness in things evil.' [32]

This statement has been widely quoted with approval, and the attitude that Shakespeare is the poet of tolerance, of 'indulgence,' appears in the criticism of Dowden, Bradley, Croce, and many more—most conspicuously perhaps in that of Raleigh, who makes quite a plea even for Pompey of *Measure for Measure*, 'one of those humble, cheerful beings, willing to help in anything that is going forward, who are the mainstay of human affairs.' [33] Since Pompey is a factotum in a house of prostitution, the praise throws a somewhat ambiguous light on 'human affairs.' Although Hazlitt's definition of the moralist as one who finds out 'the bad in everything' is scarcely philosophical, we can understand what he means, and concede that Shakespeare gives us ample scope to think kindly of sinners. The interesting point is that he satisfies a man like Johnson because, although not a moralist, he is moral; and he satisfies a man like Hazlitt because, although moral, he is not a moralist. He glides between Scylla and Charybdis. And we may note that the 'pedantic moralists' themselves do not feel repudiated by Shakespeare. The Catholics wish him of their communion,[34] and the Protestants, both of church [35] and chapel,[36] accord him the highest praise· So also does the expositor of an ethical system requiring no religious sanctions.[37]

Shakespeare sticks to the 'high road of life.' Adultery and murder are depicted as bad, fidelity and kindness as good. But it needs no moralist to tell us these things, and Shakespeare is not a moralist. A moralist has to decide, not that murder is bad and kindness is good, but what things are worst and what things are best. He must establish a hierarchy of the vices and virtues to aid us in inescapable dilemmas—in choices, not between good and bad, but between two goods and two evils. What are the competing claims of justice and mercy in a particular instance? When does the merciful act become the injurious precedent? When may a principle be sacrificed? When does an end justify a means? Which has the greater claim upon a faithful man, his lawful king or his own rebellious kinsman? And what if the king is unjust? These matters have nothing to do with 'antipathies' as Hazlitt assumes, but with 'sympathies,' and yet they are the prime concern of the moralist. Shakespeare constantly and deliberately poses these questions, and not to answer them or even to clarify their terms. Those who consider *Coriolanus* aristocratic find themselves with an embarrassing aristocrat on their hands, and those who find it democratic are left with an equally embarrassing mob. To say that Shakespeare wishes to point out that the problems are difficult is like saying he wishes to point out that murder is bad. We knew as much

already. On every point that is in the least degree debatable, his plays argue both sides. To judge them as we
would judge the writings of a moralist would be to condemn them as incompetent or unscrupulous.

Sometimes, from a moralistic point of view, the term
'unscrupulous' seems scarcely too strong. Adam of Lodge's
Rosalynde is heroic and stout, but Adam of *As You Like
It* is old and saintly, offering up his life's savings of five
hundred crowns to Orlando in the faith that He who
'providently caters for the sparrow' [38] will be the comfort
of his age. The flight of Adam and Orlando becomes a
little apologue of fidelity, mutual sacrifice, Christian kindness. But when the occasion is finished, so also is Adam.
In Lodge he is rewarded at the end with the captaincy of
the king's guards, but in Shakespeare he is discarded after
Act II when Orlando no longer needs an interlocutor, and
whether he finds comfort in his age or even receives back
his five hundred crowns is left to the conscience of the
audience. Reasons will be pointed out why Shakespeare
sometimes fails to punish the bad, but his failure to reward
the good in a case like this, leaving the example 'to operate by chance,' seems the result of sheer forgetfulness.
Evidence of his irresponsibility in matters of fact, or indifference to the implications of the facts he requisitioned,
is scattered copiously through his work. The ruinous
weather of 1595 that was bringing famine and poverty
to England provides the substance of a fancy about Oberon
and Queen Titania.[39] He so opens himself to the reproach
of rival playwrights for dealing cavalierly with the hal-
lowed memory of Sir John Oldcastle that he is forced to

apologize.[40] He lets the Earl of Cambridge appear as a traitorous and penitent foil to the great Henry the Fifth,[41] although in an earlier play he had represented him as a martyr to the cause of Mortimer.[42] Agrippa in *Antony and Cleopatra* tells us that Antony

> . . . wept
> When at Philippi he found Brutus slain,[43]

but Antony himself says

> . . . 'twas I
> That the mad Brutus ended—[44]

and both accounts contradict what had actually occurred at Philippi in Shakespeare's own earlier depiction of the scene. Then, Antony considered Brutus not mad but eminently sane, 'the elements so mixed in him . . .' and so on.[45] What was owing the memory of the historical Oldcastle, or Cambridge, or Brutus, or the rest does not seem to have concerned Shakespeare very much. For him, indeed, 'the truest poetry is the most feigning.'[46] Often Shakespeare, like Agamemnon welcoming the enemy Hector, considers that

> What's past and what's to come is strew'd
>   with husks
> And formless ruin of oblivion,[47]

and sacrifices everything, truth included, to the 'extant moment.' Who would suspect while reading the grandly chivalric and religious speeches of Bolingbroke and Mowbray of *Richard the Second*, in the opening scene and at the

Coventry lists,[48] that Shakespeare knew both of them to be sturdy liars, and King Richard their judge the worst of the three? It is wonderfully stirring while it lasts.

Matthew Arnold conferred upon Shakespeare his most magnificent award, 'high seriousness,' [49] but in a context almost impossible to interpret, and he stands alone among the more philosophical critics of the dramatist. According to Johnson, Shakespeare 'sacrifices virtue to convenience' and is 'much more careful to please than to instruct.' [50] The most original and illuminating pages of Schlegel's critique are those in which he comments on 'the secret irony of the characterization' as 'the grave of enthusiasm,' and on the signals from the playwright that he could 'unrelentingly annihilate the beautiful and irresistibly attractive scenes which his magic pen has produced.' [51] Hazlitt's statement that in *King Lear* Shakespeare was 'most in earnest' [52] reveals the critic's consciousness that elsewhere Shakespeare was less in earnest. Emerson goes so far as to quote the Koran against him.

He was the master of the revels to mankind. . . . Are the agents of nature, and the power to understand them, worth no more than a street serenade, or the breath of a cigar? One remembers again the trumpet-text in the Koran—'The heavens and the earth, and all that is between them, think ye we created them in jest?' [53]

Santayana cancels his own analysis of *Hamlet* by asking at last if the Prince's behavior is only 'a vacillation useful for theatrical purposes,' [54] and asserts that 'Even in a Hamlet, a Prospero or a Jaques, in a Henry VI or an Isabella, the poet feels no inner loyalty to the conclusion he rehearses.'[55]

49

And then there is Tolstoy's agonized protest: *'one sees that he is not in earnest, but that he is playing with words.'* [56]

An absence of moral earnestness is implied in Wright's praise of his artistic shrewdness: 'When Othello comes to murder Desdemona, "It is the cause, it is the cause, my soul," that actuates him, and his next words are "Let me not name it." He has given us, not an explanation of the cause, but a text to set a hundred critics arguing about it.' [57] Wilson makes a similar point, that Shakespeare may have 'left the question of Falstaff's cowardice as a problem to be debated,' and gives his commentary an openly commercial twist, fancying Shakespeare as replying to any queries 'with a glance and a smile at Heminge, the business manager, "Come again, gentlemen, tomorrow afternoon, and you will see." The world has been coming again and again ever since—and the debate continues.' [58]

Robert Bridges has faced most squarely, and with the most interesting and, to him, most unexpected results, the question of Shakespeare's irresponsibility. His method in treating Macbeth's motives, says Bridges, is intended 'not so much to reveal as to confuse':

The case may be boldly put thus: it would not be untrue to the facts as presented by Shakespeare to precede the drama with a scene in which Macbeth and Lady Macbeth should in Machiavellian composure deliberate together upon the murder of Duncan: but plainly such a scene would destroy the drama.

Now this veiled confusion of motive is so well managed that it must be recognized as a device intended to escape observation. That the main conception of the play is magnificent is amply proved by the effects obtained; but they are none the less procured by a deception, a liberty of treatment or a 'dishonesty,' which is purposely blurred.[59]

Deliberately, the critic points out, much matter is left 'half determined'; Shakespeare considered conduct 'to be dramatically more effective when not adequately motived'; his only object was to produce in the audience a *'pleasurable excitement.'*

Bridges submitted his essay for publication with reluctance, evidently conceiving it to be an exposure. At one time, the present writer felt a certain resentment at the critic's indictment of the audience as responsible for 'preventing the greatest poet and dramatist of the world from being the best artist,' but recognizes now that Bridges was placing the blame, if blame it must be called, precisely where it belongs. He is saying that audiences wish to be pleased—to receive 'pleasurable excitement'—and is confirming Johnson's verdict that Shakespeare was 'much more careful to please than to instruct.' In his manner of using the word *artist*, Bridges is proclaiming his personal creed; for him the artist is not one who goes to the people to give pleasure, but one to whom the people come to receive light. In a word, he is discovering that Shakespeare is not a *moralist*, and is recoiling from his discovery in dismay.

Professor Stoll has been accused so unjustly of lacking humor, aestheic sensitivity, and the like, that one hesitates to indulge in further *ad hominem* comments on this most distinguished commentator. But one suspects that fundamentally Professor Stoll is a moral idealist, a man of principle, and has never become reconciled to the fact that the poet he loves so much is not a man of principle. Stoll's discussion of Shylock and Falstaff and Hamlet suggests battles in a continuing compaign, not as he supposes against psychologizing, but against the critical tendency mentioned earlier to make Shakespeare the poet of indulgence. Cruelty and cowardice are not to be indulged, but shuddered at and mocked. Hamlet is a man of action, for the slothful cannot be loved. The tendency to shy away from character analysis may be linked to the fact that, gazed at too intently, the characterization proves morally ambiguous. Professor Stoll would rather consider Shakespeare incompetent than unscrupulous, and says revealingly on one occasion, 'His dialectic is not equal to the passions he arouses,' [61] thus assuming that Shakespeare has a dialectic—would be a good moralist if he could.

Bridges concludes his indictment of the audience by quoting the epilogue to *The Tempest:* 'My project . . . was to please.' Truly, Shakespeare admitted, here and everywhere that occasion required, that his purpose was only to please. He thinks of himself as a caterer, and shows a solicitude for the digestions of his listeners. After putting Falstaff into two plays, he begins to wonder if the audience may be 'too much cloy'd with fat meat.' [62] He promises in another to provide 'gentle pass' across the seas to France—

We'll not offend one stomach with our play.[63]

Of Shakespeare's art, this is descriptive indeed! There are the ancient words of Horace:

The poet's aim is either to profit or to please, or to blend in one the delightful and the useful . . . ; the man who mingles the useful with the sweet carries the day by charming his reader and at the same time instructing him. That's the book to enrich the publisher, to be posted overseas, and to prolong its author's fame.[64]

The hundreds who have debated which takes precedence, the profit or the pleasure, have usually treated as an irrelevance Horace's concluding revelation of the poet's aim—success. It is of the nature of the case that he occupy himself with effective means rather than with a nice consideration of ends. He is confronted by human beings who have moral interests and an appetite for pleasure. In the theatre, if not in the church, the forum, and the academy, the appetite for pleasure dominates, but it does not nullify those moral interests. Furthermore, a dramatist's materials—human behavior—are, as distinct from those of the musician and, to a large extent, the plastic artist, moral to begin with. What he must do is utilize the moral nature of his audience to satisfy its appetite for pleasure. And the way to please by moral means is to conform with prevailing moral convictions.

Shakespeare's drama is a highroad leading nowhere. It is designed as an amusement, a recreation, and therefore has no destination. It is a quality of journeys taken for amusement, by excursion boat, Ferris wheel, roller coaster, or carrousel, that they return us after their excitements to the point of departure. Shakespeare's highroad is circular. The point of departure in a particular play is the moral nature of spectator or reader. Each of us begins the circuit at a slightly different point, but when the stimulating journey is over, each finds himself at his place of departure. The play is as moral as the person who traverses its course, and exercises the good in that person to the limit of his capacities, but it intensifies his moral convictions rather than alters or extends them. The distinction between Shakespeare's plays and most modern fiction is that the plays are artistry whereas modern fiction is morality. The serious work of our time entices us on a journey that leads somewhere. Whether it advocates a new principle or, as is more common, attacks an old one, it strives to leave us elsewhere than at our starting point. We look about in confusion for our familiar moorings. As is never the case in reading Shakespeare, we come back *burdened*. We discover perhaps that we now have millions of underprivileged American Negroes on our conscience, and although we recognize that this is precisely where they belong, we feel somehow betrayed. The carrousel has proved to be a one-way train into a depressed community. Such a work deserves the highest praise as morality, and such works as a class may do the race much good provided the individual can survive them. If a note of petulance enters these remarks, it is not because of the ubiquity of moralists. We need them badly and should rejoice at their canny adoption of methods. Our complaint is not that moralists have become so many but that the artists have become so few. This purposive fiction, in novel and drama, barricades us with mountainous tasks, but gives little instruction of how the tasks are to be performed. We need the respite which artistry offers, and if we tire of its trivial forms in cinema and mystery tales, we must return to artists like Shakespeare.

To say that Shakespearean drama is a highroad leading nowhere is not paradoxical praise, once we recognize that *nowhere* means *home*—the fundamental convictions of men. Logically, one's estimate of this drama should be about as high as one's estimate of our humankind. Shakespeare himself did not underestimate. Those who admire his work but despise the 'generality' to whom it was shaped, are suffering from some kind of social-spiritual maladjustment:

'Whoever pays the cash,' said Serlio in *Wilhelm Meisters Lehrjahre,* 'may require the ware according to his liking.'
'Doubtless, in some degree,' replied his friend; 'but a great public should be reverenced, not used as children are when peddlers wish to hook the money from them.' [65]

Great critics like Aristotle and Longinus have voiced their respect for great auditories, and great artists like Molière and Goethe and Hugo have done likewise. It is the lesser critics and lesser artists who have shown aloofness or contempt. Shakespeare's drama *in toto* attests his high regard for his audience. Its most fundamental beliefs evoke his grandest utterances.

Let us consider what the highroad leading nowhere consists of in *King Lear*. Here evil is not comfortingly localized as in *Macbeth* and *Othello*. There is no mere villain with his accomplice but a league of villainy entrenched in high places. Evil is an octopus with strong and far-reaching tentacles. Good, therefore, must be correspondingly strong. In the marvelous opening scene **Cordelia's** truth shines against the falsity of her sisters, **France's** generosity against the mean calculation of **Burgundy,** Kent's selfless outburst of angry indignation against the egotism of the man he wishes to save. The acts of goodness are accompanied by immediate loss to the good, immediate gain to the evil, boding disintegration for the kind of world where men may continue to live. Yet, how goodness shines! The acts of Cordelia, then Kent, then France are like a torch passed from hand to hand, and held aloft in encroaching darkness. But what is the final issue? The good and evil go side by side to destruction.

'Ripeness is all,'[66] says Edgar, and his word is invested by some with comforting meanings—wisdom, maturity, acquiescence. But elsewhere in Shakespeare, we hear that 'we ripe and ripe . . . and then we rot and rot,'[67] and Edgar seems only to have said that man's destiny is to fall from the branch. Bradley sees on Lear's dying face an expression of ineffable joy,[68] and many have heard in the very silences of the conclusion a postulation of life after death. Others see virtue crowned with transcendental values, unrelated to benefits to anyone, here or hereafter —not a popular notion certainly, however stirring it may sound. All such ideas are in *King Lear* for anyone predisposed to detect them, but there is something else which no one can possibly miss. One can see a father and his daughter, their arms touching in the London twilight, ready to trudge let us say to Hackney, or to step in their private barge for the brief voyage to Whitehall Stairs. They know what the play was about. It is a terrible thing, perhaps the most terrible of all things, when a father turns against his own child, or the child against its own father. They knew this before they came to the theatre, Shakespeare knew that they did, and he has left them in firm possession of a truth which life, infinitely more powerful than art as a teacher, has taught them. He has given their homely truth a wonderful, a beautiful investiture.

It is time to change the metaphor and end the chapter. Shakespeare is a dramatic artist, and the relation of dramatic art to the moral nature of man is about that of wind to the surface of water. It keeps the surface agitated, spanking it into sunny little ripples or driving it into powerful surges, but it does not trouble the depths. Dramatic art neither raises nor lowers the level, and the business of the dramatic artist is to know the height of the surface upon which he works.

CHAPTER IV

INVOLVEMENT

It is always somewhat offensive to peer behind a screen. It is especially so in the realm of art because the realm is composed of screens, their surfaces lovingly designed to attract and hold our gaze. Little harm, however, is done when we peer behind that of Shakespeare. The framework we see is sturdy stuff, easily forgiven and forgotten when we resume our proper place and look at the enthralling surface intended for our eyes. We must deal now with the specific devices used by the dramatist to induce in us moral excitement—pleasurable in its effect because of attendant reassurances which will be dealt with later on.

That Shakespeare never confused 'the eternal line of separation between good and evil,'[1] that in him 'vice never walked, as it were, in twilight,'[2] and that 'good and evil are not, as today, confused or merged, but are, as Croce says "as light opposed to darkness"'[3] might be illustrated by many beautiful passages:

> Angels are bright still though the brightest fell.
> Though all things foul would wear the brows of grace,
> Yet grace must still look so.[4]

When Emilia suggests that wives retaliate upon their sinning husbands by imitating the sins, Desdemona dismisses her,

Good night, good night. Heaven me such uses send,
Not to pick bad from bad, but by bad mend! [5]

Virtue is so easily distinguishable that the vicious can be entrusted with the task of describing it to the audience. Those who wish for his death speak of Gloucester as

. . . the shepherd of the flock,
That virtuous prince, the good Duke Humphrey.[6]

Claudius describes Hamlet as 'most generous, and free from all contriving,'[7] and Iago Othello as 'of a constant, loving, and noble nature.'[8] Cassius gloats over his success in enticing Brutus into the conspiracy, 'For who so firm that cannot be seduc'd?'[9] but in the end it is Cassius himself who is seduced by Brutus's nobility. Sometimes evil is described as a threat to our faith in good, as when Imogen says,

All good seeming
By thy revolt, O husband, shall be thought
Put on for villainy.[10]

In similar terms, King Henry the Fifth describes the dereliction of Lord Scroop,[11] and Troilus that of Cressida,[12] but only in the frenzied minds of the disillusioned, a Timon or a Lear, is the threat fulfilled.

Nevertheless, it must be noted that the distinction between good and evil in the plays is predicated upon a pre-existing distinction between good and evil in the minds of the spectators. Both vice and virtue *do* 'walk in twilight'— but twilight not quite too deep for the keenness of our

59

eyes; and good and evil, although not confused, are ever intermingled. There are plenty of texts for the sophist:

> There is some soul of goodness in things evil,
> Would men observingly distil it out,[13]

says Henry the Fifth; and Friar Laurence completes the equation:

> Virtue itself turns vice, being misapplied,
> And vice sometime's by action dignified.[14]

And just as good and evil are interpenetrable, so are they relative. Hamlet says, 'there is nothing either good or bad but thinking makes it so,'[15] and Aufidius adds his testimony, 'our virtues lie in the interpretations of the times.'[16] These are casual remarks by perplexed characters; still, the idea that vice and virtue are not absolutes, and that excessive virtue becomes vice, is one of the commonest in Shakespeare. It is exemplified in the characterization of a King Henry the Sixth, a Malvolio, and an Angelo in varying degrees of seriousness. It is voiced by villainous Claudius,

> . . . goodness, growing to a plurisy,
> Dies in his own too-much.[17]

as well as by the holy anchorite of St. Francis. It underlies the tolerance of a Helena for a Parolles,

> . . . fix'd evils sit so fit in him
> That they take place when virtue's steely bones
> Look bleak i' th' cold wind.[18]

and is boldly stated by Mariana,

They say best men are moulded out of faults
And, for the most part, become much more the better
For being a little bad.[19]

This is parlously near to Samuel Butler's fancy in *Erewhon*, of men repenting the good they have 'committed' and increasing in amiability as they decrease in virtue.

The commonest of all presentations of good and evil in Shakespeare is in juxtaposition. The two stand constantly side by side in a single play, a single situation, a single person—forming a character like Bertram's, 'of a mingled yarn, good and ill together.'[20] One is inclined to say that Shakespeare mingles good and bad in his characters because he imitates life; and Professor Wright has cogently argued that it is by inconsistency that he creates his illusion of reality.[21] In other writers there is more consistency and less illusion. 'And indeed,' says Morgann, in the earliest analysis of the matter, 'this clear perception, in Novels and Plays, of the union of character and action not seen in nature, is the principal defect of such compositions, and what renders them but ill pictures of human life, and wretched guides of conduct.'[22] But in many ways Shakespeare is far from being realistic, and the question remains of why he should have been true to life in this particular and not in others. The faults of a Lear, a Hamlet, or an Othello have reminded critics of Aristotle's dictum that the character of a tragic hero should be better than his actions; there has been much discussion of tragic guilt or fatal 'flaws.' But we are left with an uneasy awareness that Shakespeare's methods in creating a Hamlet or a Lear are only an extension of his methods in creating all the other

characters, and that in comedy and history as well as tragedy the characters have 'flaws'—usually left unchastised.
Shakespeare did not distribute defects in order to have
something to punish.

The clue seems to lie in the greater stimulant effect of
the mixed character. Pictures of Christian struggling with
Apollyon are interesting only for their composition. They
have no moral interest. Christian is good, Apollyon bad,
and that is the end of it. But Claudius, Gertrude, and
Hamlet require constant evaluation on our part. We have
to keep weighing them on our scales. Always in Shakespeare we perceive that the good might be better and the
bad might be worse, and we are excited by our perceptions.
The virtuous seem to need our counsel, and the vicious
seem capable of understanding our censure. We are linked
to the former by sensations of solicitude, and to the latter
by moments of sympathy and understanding. We are constantly *involved*.

It is commonplace observation that Shakespeare uses
every hue except black and white. That Coriolanus, so
noble, pure-spirited, and brave, is ruinously arrogant is
obvious to all: 'He wants nothing of a god but eternity
and a heaven to throne in,' [23] says one of his fellow characters. But the more interesting point is that Coriolanus fails
to give complete satisfaction even on his heroical side. He
has been called 'a great boy,' and Professor Campbell has
dwelt in detail on his subservience to his mother.[24] It is
difficult not to see a humorous intention in the inventory
of his wounds.[25] That the play *Julius Caesar* is properly
named, that it is dominated by the conqueror's great spirit

is often maintained. 'O Julius Caesar, thou are mighty yet!' [26] is the text supplied by the dramatist to those who advance the view. Yet we must admit that there is something in the Shakespearean portrait at least partially justifying Charlton's conception of Caesar as a hen-pecked pantaloon.[27] Shaw tells us that Shakespeare wrote Caesar down in order to write Brutus up.[28] But Brutus is written 'up' only to a point. His virtues as a husband, his kindness as a master, his sentiment for friendship—

> My heart doth joy that yet in all my life
> I found no man but he was true to me—[29]

are Shakespeare's additions to Plutarch; but so also, in almost equal measure, are Brutus's stiffness, lack of humor, fastidiousness—what MacCallum calls his 'cult of perfection.' [30] And the treachery involved in the slaying of Caesar is finally given eloquent expression in the mouths of Caesar's friends.[31] The character of Timon of Athens is not a subtle one. That Timon never knew the 'middle of humanity' but the 'extremity of both ends' [32] is glaringly illustrated by such contrasting speeches as—

O what a precious comfort 'tis to have so many like brothers commanding one another's fortunes! O, joy's e'en made away ere't can be born! Mine eyes cannot hold out water, methinks.[33]

and

> . . . show charity to none
> But let the famish'd flesh slide from the bone
> Ere thou relieve the beggar. Give to dogs
> What thou deniest to men.[34]

What we seem to have in the play as it stands is an unfinished portrait, the contrasting colors of which still lie raw on the canvas. Had the play been brought to the perfection of the other tragedies, there would have been something of the cynic in the earlier Timon, something of the sentimentalist in the later one, or at least a toning down of effects until the play lost its explicit quality and intimated rather than proclaimed that its hero acted 'unwisely, not ignobly.' [35] In the case of Mark Antony, there is majesty even in self-indulgence. Although he invites 'full surfeits and the dryness of his bones' [36] and seeks consolation for disgrace in 'one other gaudy night,' [37] the exhibition never achieves the disgusting. We cannot withhold all admiration from a man who cries,

> Let Rome in Tiber melt and the wide arch
> Of the rang'd empire fall! Here is my space.[38]

And at the end we agree, although with the inevitable note of reservation,

> No grave upon the earth shall clip in it
> A pair so famous.[39]

The role of Desdemona is one of the most remarkable in Shakespeare. No woman in the plays is more pure than she, none whose every word is so compounded of kindliness, purity, and faith; and yet the aura of suspicion surrounding her is not purely of Iago's creation. Desdemona has married a Moor. About Othello's physical qualities we are left in no doubt. He is called 'thick-lips' and 'an old black ram.' [40] Elsewhere in Shakespeare, a black skin is viewed as revolting or as a symbol of evil.[41] Aaron's thick lips and woolly hair are stigmata, and even his babe is described as 'loathsome as a toad.' [42] The Prince of Morocco, like Othello, is permitted to show pride in his race,[43] but for Portia he has 'the complexion of a devil,' [44] and she is happy when he goes away. Shakespeare retained the black skin of Cinthio's character and added a further disabling feature—middle-age. In his own words, Othello is declined 'into the vale of years.' [45] In the popular mind of Shakespeare's time as of today the attraction of an Othello for a Desdemona would have only one explanation—the waywardness of lust; Hamlet's most virulent attack upon his mother is informed with suspicion and disgust provoked by the ugliness of Claudius.[46] Another suspicion attaching to Desdemona at the outset arises from the deception she has practiced upon her father. All Shakespeare's maidens in love deceive their fathers (except Ophelia), but only Desdemona's is permitted to speak as Brabantio speaks,

> Look to her, Moor, if thou hast eyes to see.
> She has deceiv'd her father, and may thee.[47]

We may say that the speech serves to sow a seed in Othello's mind, but it also sows one in ours. Cinthio tells us directly that in marrying a Moor the lady was 'not drawn by female appetite.' [48] Shakespeare makes no such apology. Instead Iago is permitted to harp upon the theme with terrible vividness:

> Foh! one may smell in such a will most rank,
> Foul disproportion, thoughts unnatural—[49]

Shakespeare counters both Iago's charges and our predisposition in the matter by changing the Moor from the stealthy assassin he is in Cinthio to a man a pure woman might love, and by elevating Desdemona to the point of idealization.

Shakespeare's villains are not wholly villainous—even the fearful three of *King Lear*. Edmund has provocation for his deeds, and unlike his prototype, in the story of the Paphlagonian unkind king by Sidney,[50] does not himself blind his father. Edmund is capable of pity,[51] and dies attempting to do a kindness.[52] This leaves Goneril and Regan as 'the only pictures of the . . . pure unnatural' [53] in Shakespeare. But Regan is not so bad as Goneril, and thus shades off from black to dark-grey; and there are moments when we see eye to eye even with Goneril. In her objections to the riot of her father's train she at least acts understandably,[54] and were it not for the exceptional nature of the situation would be wholly in the right. It requires an effort of the imagination on our part to side at this moment with Lear, who, in his curse upon his daughter's fertility,[55] seems less sinned against than sinning. Goneril and Regan at first feel the need of self-justification [56]—are not devoid of conscience. It is not until Act III, Scene 7, that they appear as hell-hounds. Sympathy with Lear in the interim from Act II has so taken possession of us that any touches of humanity in the daughters would now seem an irrelevance, and Shakespeare does not wastefully or confusingly include them. The earlier touches served their purpose. They distributed the onus of guilt between Lear and his daughters, and kept us alert measuring the rights of the case as it then appeared. Outside of *King Lear*, Shakespeare's blackest characters are King Richard the Third and Iago, but neither is a picture of pure malignance. The trigger-men in modern gangster films are more dreadful, more troll-like, and an Elmer Gantry is much more disgusting. Shakespeare the artist, unlike Lewis the moralist, declines to disgust. Richard and Iago, like Pecksniff and Squeers and Uriah Heep, are amusing devils—at least until the moment their deviltry bears fruit in human suffering. There is then little time left to loathe them. In the meanwhile, their very devotion to wickedness, their energy and vivacity, is exhilarating, and we are entertained by their actions as by the action in *Candide*. Cruelty cannot be made amusing, but neither Richard nor Iago seems enamored of cruelty so much as of self-expression. Richard wishes to dominate and Iago to be clever.

Characters like King Richard the Third and Iago are neither so common nor characteristic as King Richard the Second, whom we rarely classify as a villain at all. Yet what a sad offender he is! He cruelly insults dying Gaunt and seizes his property. He is treacherous to friends at home; and to enemies abroad he basely yields 'upon compromise' what 'his ancestors fought for.' [57] He indulges his pleasures and pillages the realm, losing the hearts of both commons and nobles. His self-pity is egregious, and he speaks of himself as of Christ. If we look for the opposite of Henry the Fifth, who is virtuous and strong, we will find him in neither Richard the Third, who is strong if not virtuous, nor in Henry the Sixth, who is virtuous if not strong, but in the indescribable Richard the Second, who is neither strong nor virtuous. He is the eternally immature, the living lie, the kind who attracts, sucks dry, and passes on, leaving a weakened faith in generous human responses because of the way he frustrates them. How indignant we ought to be with him! Yet we rarely are. Shakespeare's worst king is never hated, and is often even loved—for his eloquence, his irresponsibility amounting almost to innocence, his deep conviction that he is *deserving* of love. Those who dethrone him speak of him later as that 'sweet lovely Rose.' [58]

Shakespeare often, as in *Hamlet*, finds the disparate elements which serve his purpose in the pre-existing legend. An interesting illustration is provided by the character of Macbeth. Holinshed portrays Macbeth when a subject as—

cruel of nature . . . a bloudie tyrant, & a cruell murtherer of them whome the kings mercie had pardoned. . . .[59]

but Macbeth as king as—

the sure defense and buckler of innocent people; and hereto he also applied his whole indeuor, to cause yoong men to exercise themselves in vertuous maners, and men of the church to attend their diuine service according to their vocations. . . .

Confronted by this dual personality, Holinshed effects a *rapprochement*—

But this was but a counterfet zeale of equitie shewed by him, partlie against his naturall inclination to purchase thereby the fauour of the people.[60]

Shakespeare acts upon the suggestion of the dual personality but discards the *rapprochement*. Whatever else he may be, Shakespeare's Macbeth is not a hypocrite. His two personalities are both authentic, and stand unreconciled throughout the play. Like Faustus, he repents before he sells his soul, while he sells his soul, and after he sells his soul. Dripping with the blood of the innocent, he can still say to Macduff,

> Of all men else I have avoided thee.
> But get thee back! My soul is too much charg'd
> With blood of thine already.[61]

Macbeth is good man and a bad man. He is ourselves with our personal devils. His story has for us the fearful fascination of those dreams in which we have murdered men.

If Shakespeare does not find a disparity in his sources, he creates one. An instance is supplied by King Henry the Fourth's unfulfilled resolution to lead a crusade to the Holy Lands. In Holinshed this resolution is treated as pure idealism:

For it greeued him to consider the great malice of christian princes, that were bent vpon a mischeefous purpose to destroie one another, to the perill of their owne soules, rather than to make war against the enimies of the christian faith, as in conscience (it seemed to him) they were bound.[62]

Shakespeare's Henry the Fourth, in contrast, has two reasons for planning a crusade:

69

To chase these pagans in those holy fields
Over whose acres walk'd those blessed feet
Which fourteen hundred years ago were nail'd
For our advantage on the bitter cross.[63]

and this—

I cut them off [his nobles], and had a purpose now
To lead out many to the Holy Land,
Lest rest and lying still might make them look
Too near my state.[64]

The effect of these two speeches, when placed side by side, is appalling. But Shakespeare does not place them side by side, and it cannot be too greatly stressed that the speaker's self-contradiction is not overt. King Henry the Fourth simply has *two* reasons for going to the Holy Lands. His son has two reasons for frequenting the Boar's Head Tavern: it is educational and it is amusing. We may say that hypocrisy runs in the family, but Shakespeare does not say so. Any tendency to make the two reasons one, or to reject the first and accept the second or vice versa, he leaves to us. The third member of the succession, King Henry the Sixth, is presented as saintly and spineless, and neither quality cancels out the other.

It is needless to multiply illustrations. The moral duality of Shakespeare's characters does not give them the complexity of living men, but it does distinguish them from most characters of literature. Master Page of Windsor is the right kind of husband but the wrong kind of father. Caliban is a brute but a sensitive brute. Jack Cade is the 'filth and scum of Kent' [65] but a man of pride. Capulet is an arbitrary and irascible parent but provides for his daughter a suitor above reproach. Always there is some barrier to our complete condemnation or complete approval of a character—something to keep us exercised. Since the marriage of King Henry the Eighth and Anne Bullen is favorably presented, we should expect the discarded Queen Katherine to be portrayed as a shrew; and Sir Edmund Chambers actually complains that something of the kind is not done.[66] But as a matter of fact Shakespeare goes far beyond Holinshed in giving Katherine virtue and ability, and he movingly dramatizes her distress. To pit good against bad is to stage a less equal and less interesting match than to pit good against good. Shakespeare's design was not to celebrate Anne Bullen but to involve his audience.

The stimulant effect of non-homogeneous characters may be briefly illustrated. Among plays such as Shakespeare's, *The Tempest* is not outstanding, and the first few hundred lines of the second act not especially remarkable. These lines pave the way for an averted assassination. There are six speaking characters: Alonso, the prospective victim; Gonzalo, his faithful minister, who will prevent the crime; Sebastian and Antonio, who will attempt it; and Adrian and Francisco, who will be mere pawns. To be prepared for their various actions we must be made acquainted with their 'characters.' Gonzalo must be shown as *good*, Sebastian and Antonio as *bad*, and Alonso as so overcome with grief for his lost son as to be momentarily defenseless. All quite easy—and, as we might readily imagine, quite uninteresting.

But in Shakespeare these characters all have an alloy. Gonzalo's goodness is a little egregious. He is kindly, but boringly optimistic, and importunate in his consolations which, as always in Shakespeare, are ill-received. Sebastian and Antonio are cynical and malicious, but they are clever and amusing. The weakness of Gonzalo they clearly perceive, and their comments upon him have a barb which he fumblingly attempts to counter. Gonzalo outlines his ideal commonwealth. Its weakness is that it reckons not with the defects of human nature. Sebastian and Antonio are aware of this weakness, the more so that they themselves are such people as would make a Utopia impossible. The pure and impractical is brought into juxtaposition with the practical and impure. As the scene progresses, we spectators find our own moral natures more and more involved. We have laughed a little at Gonzalo's virtue—have identified ourselves a little with the mockers and scorners. To the extent that we have done so we are implicated in their vice. Our debt to virtue has accrued sufficiently that it is no longer a matter of indifference that the assassination be averted: the crime in a measure would be ours.

Chapter V

PARADOXES

Falstaff is the most popular creation of Elizabethan drama. He is the only character for whom his creator had to devise a special play, and *The Merry Wives of Windsor* must be viewed as a command performance whether or not the command came from the Queen. In the seventeenth century, there are five allusions to Falstaff for every one to Hamlet, and about seven for every one to Morose, the most frequently mentioned character in the plays of Jonson. These references to Falstaff are distinguished from those to other characters by their tone of 'affectionate familiarity.'[1] His fame has never diminished. Falstaff, in the eighteenth century, was the subject of the first public lecture ever given on Shakespeare,[2] and of the first really impressive piece of interpretive criticism.[3] He is the subject of the latest book by the most popular Shakespearean critic of our own day.[4] Although Hugo calls Falstaff 'centaur man and pig,'[5] Taine, a man with the 'passions of an animal,'[6] Tolstoy, 'a repulsive character,'[7] and Stoll protests against letting him dissolve into 'airy nothings' all 'that makes life real and earnest,'[8] theirs is distinctly a minority report. Dr. Johnson, although he had sternly reprehended his corruption of a prince, felt nostalgia while reading *King Henry the Fifth* for 'unimitated, unimitable Falstaff'[9] and his rag-tag crew—'I believe every reader regrets their departure' [10]—and from the time of Morgann and Schlegel until the present, critics in overwhelming majority have proclaimed their attachment to the vastbellied knight. And all this in spite of his being the exemplar of every detestable vice!

Sir Walter Raleigh, as fond as the next man of Falstaff, once remarked in another connection that an Englishman can tolerate any form of evil except cruelty and 'bilking' [11] —that is, cheating the helpless. But Falstaff cruelly sends misfits into battle, and, as Dame Quickly or Ralph Mouldy could testify, he is a merciless 'bilker.' He is bully, toady, grafter, lecher, drunkard, glutton, liar, slanderer, hypocrite, parasite, thief—and possibly a coward.

Discussions of whether Falstaff is or is not a coward always strike us as applying to someone other than Falstaff, but it is thus that we have to begin. Certainly he is not presented as a man of valor. He runs away roaring at Gad's Hill, and he plays dead on the battlefield of Shrewsbury. Such acts, however, may or may not indicate cowardice, for cowardice cannot be diagnosed from superficial symptoms. A man who leaps out of the way of a falling tree is no coward. If he is a fat man who roars as he leaps, his loss of dignity will be comic. 'How you did jump!' his friends will cry, and their taunts will sound as if directed at cowardice although such is not truly the case; they would not have had their companion act otherwise than as he did. From the point of view of either society or the individual there is no sense in letting oneself be crushed by a falling tree. No moral principle is involved. Cowardice enters the picture only when a principle is involved. A coward is one who leaps when he ought to stand his ground. The obligation to stand one's ground, however, may be apparent to society but not to the individual. The person to whom running away from footpads or playing dead on a battlefield is like leaping away from a falling tree cannot be convicted of cowardice. *His is the larger guilt of having no principles.*

When Falstaff is taking his ease at his inn, with a doxy on his knee, drunken Pistol disturbs him. Something is threatened that the fat knight values, and now he falls to with his sword. He is proud, and a little surprised at himself: 'The rogue fled from me like quicksilver.' [12] Falstaff feels no mission to stand up against footpads or to defend his country; he does not recognize the obligation. His seems to be the larger guilt of having no principles; yet none of us are quite sure. To Falstaff a reputation for valor, if not worth fighting for, is at least worth lying for; and he sometimes expresses shame, sometimes good intentions, even when alone.[13] Furthermore, we cannot conceive of a man utterly lacking in principles directing his energies towards Falstaff's trivial ends—a Macchiavelli sponging in a pub. Thus Falstaff's outer vices divert our attention from his inner vice, the lack of principles, at the same time that this inner vice nullifies the outer vices. It is a neat trick. We call him a coward—but without conviction. So also we call him bully, toady, grafter, and the other things on the fatal list—but without conviction. He renders the terms irrelevant.

Falstaff is the least effective wrongdoer that ever lived. He is a thief whose booty is taken from him, a liar who is never believed, a drunkard who is never befuddled, a bully who is not feared, a prince's companion who sleeps on a bench in Eastcheap, a toady who misses preferment. Even his lechery is a doubtful item. Although he carries a list of bawdy houses in his pocket, and is charged with using Dame Quickly 'both in purse and in person,' [14] his attentions to Doll Tearsheet evoke a wry comment from Poins: 'Is it not strange that desire should so many years outlive performance?' [15] And the comment prepares us for what comes a little later—the most scandalous bit of byplay in Shakespeare.[16] It is true that the mortality rate among Falstaff's poor conscripts is high, but the fact is presented in no way that touches our imagination. We witness painful consequences of none of his sins. Rape and murder, the irreparable offenses, are the ones that he does not commit. Shakespeare holds him on an invisible leash. He participates a little in the rehabilitation of Prince Hal at the end of part one, but at the end of part two, his habits threaten to cease being harmless, and the leash comes taut with a jerk. Hal is now King Henry the Fifth, and Falstaff shouts in glee: 'Let us take any man's horses; the laws of England are at my commandment. Blessed are they that have been my friends, and woe to my Lord Chief Justice!' [17] Soon after, comes his *rejection*—the most royal snub in literature.

This is a most imperfect analysis of Falstaff. His endearing qualities remain untreated, the natural and human touches in his delineation, his intelligence, his gaiety and wit, the way he gives his companions value in entertainment much greater than value received, the touching precariousness of his existence prophetic of his end. He is old and fat and disreputable, with at least one trait in common with Don Quixote and Cyrano: he tilts against the world without the thick shield of prudence. No wonder that so many have muttered curses at his king. It is impossible to oversubtilize the character. To attribute to chance the effects produced is to make Shakespeare the luckiest blunderer in history. One can only quote Maurice Morgann:

> If any one thinks these observations are the effect of too much refinement, and that there was in truth more of chance in the case than of management or design, let him try his own luck;— perhaps he may draw out of the wheel of fortune a Macbeth, an Othello, a Benedict, or a Falstaff.[18]

Whatever else he is, Falstaff is a moral paradox. Like every paradox, he tickles and dazzles. 'Uncertainty and bewilderment in the individual, division and disunion in the audience,' protests Professor Stoll at our doubts about the cowardice, '—and that is the death of laughter.' [19] But truly, that is the *birth* of laughter. Morgann has been accused of confusing art and reality, although no critic has had a finer perception of their distinction. His only error, if error it be, is in placing cowardice in a separate category from the knight's other vices and in trying, playfully let us observe, to transform it into courage. Underlying the playfulness is something more serious—the interesting hypothesis that the quality of courage is indispensable to give the character cohesion; even vices must have something to which to adhere. The idea is sound, but the quality required may not be courage but simply vitality, life-force, the faculty of survival,—and Falstaff has plenty of this.

The value of Morgann's essay lies in its introduction and conclusion, which place it high above the usual treatise in aesthetics or any subsequent discussion of Falstaff. Detached at one end from malicious intent and at the other from painful effect, Falstaff's vices are shown to be mere incongruities. But consider the implications—vice the ravening beast made a mere incongruity! Here is the paradox. Vice walking on earth is a terrible thing, but vice dancing in air is a delightful novelty. We are freed from the burdens of fear and disapproval. We fondle the viper and stroke the wolf. We laugh. It is Shakespeare's intention. And let us observe this: laughing at sin can mean to a moralist nothing but sinful laughter. We can hear the voices of Jeremy Collier and the others, warning us that to treat heaven in jest is 'to go to Hell in earnest,' that 'to laugh without reason is the pleasure of fools.' [20] The words of Robert Bridges are laden with sorrow that a poet like Shakespeare should stoop to give pleasure by means such as this.[21]

Falstaff's speech attacking honor is in itself a moral paradox—

. . . what is honour? A word. What is that word honour? Air. A trim reckoning! Who hath it? He that died a Wednesday. . . .[22]

The devil's advocate is given a chance to make out the stronger case for the weaker side. Speeches of similar nature and equal length are scattered through the plays. Falstaff himself is given another quite lengthy one attacking water-drinking—

If I had a thousand sons, the first humane principle I would teach them should be to forswear thin potations and to addict themselves to sack. . . .[23] etc.

In *Love's Labour's Lost,* Berowne attacks study, but since he is not obviously an irresponsible, a kind of disclaimer is appended,

> . . . I have for barbarism spoke more
> Than for that angel knowledge you can say.[24]

In *King Richard the Third,* a bravo attacks conscience—

. . . it makes a man a coward. A man cannot steal, but it accuseth him; a man cannot swear, but it checks him; a man cannot lie with his neighbour's wife, but it detects him. 'Tis a blushing shame-fac'd spirit . . .[25] etc.

In *All's Well that Ends Well,* the clown defends cuckoldry—

If I be his cuckold, he's my drudge. He that comforts my wife is the cherisher of my flesh and blood . . .[26] etc.

And Parolles attacks virginity—

Virginity breeds mites, much like a cheese; consumes itself to the very paring, and so dies with feeding his own stomach. Besides virginity is peevish, proud, idle, made of self-love . . .[27] etc.

In *Coriolanus,* the humorous servants attack peace—

Peace is a very apoplexy, lethargy; mull'd, deaf, sleepy, insensible, a getter of more bastard children than war's a destroyer of men.[28]

We are reminded of Jaques's praise of folly, of the struggle between Launcelot Gobbo's conscience and the fiend, and of similar fooling.

The most entertaining passage in *The Two Gentlemen of Verona* is Launce's speech to his ill-mannered dog. The appeal lies not in the images of the unhousebroken animal —Shakespeare's humor is rarely scatological—but in the paradoxical setting of these images in Launce's moralistic, sadly reproachful, self-righteous words. He speaks in sorrow not in anger—'When didst thou see me heave up my leg and make water against a gentlewoman's farthingale?' [29] What a way to echo the tones of all who teach by good example! Often in Shakespeare the moral paradox—the basic ingredient in the whole conception of Falstaff—is contained in a single sally. 'What I have suffer'd,' says Falstaff himself in the role of pander, 'to bring this woman to evil for your good.' [30] Justice Shallow is obviously a religious man:

Certain, 'tis certain; very sure, very sure. Death, as the Psalmist saith, is certain to all; all shall die. How [much] a good yoke of bullocks at Stamford fair? [31]

Then there is Davy's way of obtaining justice by being a friend at court:

I grant your worship that he is a knave, sir; but yet God forbid, sir, but a knave should have some countenance at his friend's request! An honest man, sir, is able to speak for himself.[32]

And Dame Quickly's way of comforting the dying:

So 'a cried out 'God, God, God!' three or four times. Now I, to comfort him, bid him 'a should not think of God; I hop'd there was no need to trouble himself with any such thoughts yet.[33]

Or, to take the briefest possible illustration of the way moral values are made to pirouette for our delight, we have Stephano's lament for the loss of his bottle of liquor: 'There is not only *disgrace* and *dishonour* in that, monster, but an infinite *loss*.' [34]

In the world of practical affairs it would be a sad thing if we considered moral imbecility amusing. But in the Shakespearean world we are not offended that the young and virginal Juliet is entrusted to that impervious *Nurse*. An obliging creature the Nurse; she wants to see people happy; bigamy holds no terrors for her. Juliet calls her 'ancient damnation' [35] not really because of her lack of scruples but because of her expedient disparagement of Romeo. Dame Quickly is the best of all illustrations of amusing moral imbecility. She is an earnest, aspiring, conscientious soul, who in her own eyes has never lost her respectability. Appearances, she firmly believes, are being kept up, and she sees no distinction between appearances and reality. Her words have always the accent of rectitude. She reports a moral conversation between herself and the deputy—her family minister was present at the time—in a scene in which she is tippling with a prostitute.[36] She changes less between *King Henry the Fourth* and *The Merry Wives of Windsor* than does Falstaff himself. In her reincarnation as a household servant she promises to help each of the rivals for the hand of Anne Page: 'I will do what I can for them all three; for so I have promis'd, and I'll be as good as my word.' [37]

The moral paradox, reducing for the moment our values to mere coruscations, is one of the means by which Shakespeare utilizes our moral natures to afford us pleasure. Falstaff certainly serves no didactic purpose. Delight in him is a test of our normality. If we were not moral to begin with, we would not be amused. 'Unmitigated lustiness,' in Santayana's striking phrase, 'will snarl at pictures.' [38] Falstaff can provide no excitement to the animal man; and to the moral imbecile Dame Quickly's behavior would seem commonplace enough. On the other hand, Falstaff can give no pleasure to the saint, or to the one in saintly mood. The latter's hatred of sin is too all-engrossing; he cannot play with it. The saint at his best is already free, released from the pressures of fear and longing, and in no need of moments of respite. But between the morally depraved and the saints stand the multitude, including men in pulpits and men in prisons, including Shakespeare's audience of today and yesterday.

Chapter VI

ENIGMAS

Ben Jonson once expressed the opinion that Shakespeare should have blotted a thousand lines, and he submitted a sample:

Many times hee fell into those things, could not escape laughter: As when hee said in the person of *Caesar*, one speaking to him; *'Caesar, thou dost me wrong.'* Hee replyed, *'Caesar did never wrong, but with just cause;* and such like: which were ridiculous.[1]

The offensive line had actually been blotted, or altered at least, before *Julius Caesar* was printed in the Folio,[2] but that it had appeared in the original text is likely enough. We think of Bassanio's plea to Shylock's judge, 'To do a great right, do a little wrong'[3]; of Helena's finding 'lawful meaning in a wicked act'[4]; and many similar instances. Shakespeare constantly uses the moral dilemma in an experimental or provocative way. The most conspicuous case is that in which Isabella is required to choose between her chastity and her brother's life. Its very conspicuousness, however, is a reminder that in Shakespeare such dilemmas are as a rule more obliquely treated. The artistic wisdom of the oblique treatment is illustrated by the fate of *Measure for Measure*: Coleridge called it a 'hateful work'[5] and it has distressed more readers than any other Shakespearean play. As will be suggested later, Shakespeare does not really tell us how a woman ought to choose if placed in Isabella's position, but to many he appears to do so, and they are troubled by her choice. Usually his method is to leave the issue undecided, to suspend it or dissolve it, or to place the problem where we glimpse it only from the corner of our eye. Gazing at it directly must be an act of volition on our part. Any deciding vote on the rights of the case must be ours, not his. He is enigmatic, or, from a moralist's viewpoint, evasive.

Antony and Cleopatra treats in its central situation not a moral dilemma—it is no 'love-and-honor' play—but the consequences of a moral error. Antony's wife, however, faces a moral dilemma. Her husband and her brother are at war:

> The good gods will mock me presently
> When I shall pray 'O, bless my lord and husband!'
> Undo that prayer by crying out as loud
> 'O bless my brother!' Husband win, win brother,
> Prays, and destroys the prayer; no midway
> 'Twixt these extremes at all.[6]

In such difficult choices, with their tragic resolutions, a Corneille or Racine finds his central interest, but Shakespeare only glances at them. In *Coriolanus* Volumnia pleads with her beloved son, who is in arms against her beloved Rome:

> For how can we,
> Alas, how can we for our country pray,
> Whereto we are bound, together with thy victory,
> Whereto we are bound? [7]

84

The dilemma seems to dissolve when her son is persuaded to abandon his conquest. We see Volumnia welcomed in triumph to Rome, and immediately thereafter we see her son slain by those who had expected him to lead them in victory. On any causal connection between Volumnia's saving her country and her son's losing his life the play is silent.

Brutus is pictured to us as deciding whether to join the conspirators in the assassination of Caesar. By revealing his personal obligations to Caesar on the one hand, and his anti-imperialist ardor on the other—both of which are treated by Plutarch,—Shakespeare could have presented a real moral dilemma. But he chooses otherwise. To show a man as good as Brutus placing an abstract political principle above friendship and gratitude would be to give the scene the kind of clearcut advocacy on a debatable issue that Shakespeare prefers to avoid. The friendship and personal obligations are toned down, and Brutus is shown choosing to act without 'personal cause to spurn at' Caesar (indeed he has not!), but for sake of 'the general' [8]—whatever that may be—or, as we hear later, for the 'common good to all.' [9] He is a righteous man doing his duty. Without meeting difficulty head on, we find quite enough in the play—Cassius's enticements, Caesar's merits, Brutus's practical ineptitude, and the fact that the action which begins with one dictator ends with three—to make us ponder over the merits of Brutus's choice.

Shakespeare has no hesitation, in cases where personal dignity or courage is concerned—the honor of soldiers—to let estimable men see the morally superior side and choose the inferior one. What he does in such cases is to withhold condemnation from the men, but picture fully the merits of the rejected course. Then we can think as we please. Palamon and Arcite deplore the tyranny of Creon and the corruption in Thebes, but decide notwithstanding to resist the crusading Theseus. They recognize their moral status to be dubious but decide to 'leave that unreason'd.' [10] The most extended scene of this kind is that in which Hector discusses with Troilus and the rest whether to surrender Helen to the Greeks. 'Let Helen go,' says Hector, and he rebukes those who argue to keep her as

> . . . not much
> Unlike young men, whom Aristotle thought
> Unfit to hear moral philosophy.[11]

Then follows his conclusive demonstration that the—

> . . . moral laws
> Of nature and of nations speak aloud
> To have her back return'd.

But thus he concludes:

> Hector's opinion
> Is this in way of truth. Yet ne'ertheless,
> My sprightly brethren, I propend to you
> In resolution to keep Helen still;
> For 'tis a cause that hath no mean dependence
> Upon our joint and several dignities.[12]

It all seems to have been no more than an interesting debate. The possibility that Hector was mocking his brethren or was himself being mocked by the playwright is very slight: almost alone of the characters in this play he is portrayed as direct, honorable, and even kind. Occasionally a character chooses the right course of conduct but resents the obligation. When Menas offers to slay the guests who are political rivals, young Pompey forbids it but rebukes him for not killing them before asking permission.[13]

In the English historical plays, ethical dilemmas toss about like jetsam on the billows. King Henry the Sixth must choose between further civil strife and the dispossession of his son; John of Gaunt must choose between loyalty to his king and avenging his brother's murder; King Lewis must choose between

> . . . a heavy curse from Rome
> Or the light loss of England for a friend.[14]

After much ethical perplexity—representing Shakespeare's embellishments rather than anything suggested by the sources—Lewis follows the Dauphin's advice to 'forgo the easier.' It is thus that nearly everyone behaves in the historical plays. Faced by a moral alternative, the individual chooses on grounds of expediency, is overwhelmed by circumstances, or luckily released from the need of making up his mind. Usually he yields to the pressure of circumstance, goes with the drift of the times. Shakespeare constantly presents the problems, then dismisses them, with little indication of what man should do but ample indication of what he does do.

When Faulconbridge is confronted by the dead body of little Prince Arthur and the probability that the king his master is responsible for the death, he resorts to something suspiciously like bluster:

> It is a damned and a bloody work,
> The graceless action of a heavy hand
> If that it be the work of any hand.[15]

If anyone looks for the way in which the relations between king and loyal subject ought to be affected by such a situation, he will look in vain. In *King Richard the Third* Lord Stanley is offered the choice between aiding a tyrant or losing his son, but evades the necessity of doing either. *King Richard the Second* is especially rich in unresolved dilemmas. York must choose between the cause of King Richard and that of Bolingbroke:

> Both are my kinsmen.
> Th' one is my sovereign, whom both my oath
> And duty defend; t' other again
> Is my kinsman, whom the King hath wrong'd,
> Whom conscience and my kindred bids to right.
> Well, somewhat we must do.[16]

And that is as near as we come to any philosophical solution of the problem. York decides to remain 'neuter' after being divested of power to aid either side.

Sometimes the moral dilemma and its enigmatical treatment is absorbed, so to speak, in the character. The character himself then becomes an enigma. We who try to explain the behavior of Hamlet should run a trial heat by explaining the behavior of Northumberland in *King Henry the Fourth*. He is Hotspur's father and sworn ally; yet he fails to bring up the promised aid to the battlefield of

expedition against Poland, we are given a description of Ophelia's madness:

> Her speech is nothing,
> Yet the unshaped use of it doth move
> The hearers to collection; they aim at it,
> And botch the words up fit to their own thoughts.[24]

The word *Sphinx* is common in *Hamlet* criticism, and even the word *hoax* is occasionally heard. Some say that the difficulties are imaginary and the meaning perfectly clear —*their* meaning. Others view the play as an accident, resulting from a collision with some other play, probably by Thomas Kyd. And finally we are treated to a comedy turn by suave entertainers who soberly assure us that, as a matter of fact, the play is a failure. But the body of *Hamlet* criticism is so varied, copious, and fascinating that to deal with it ever so slightly would be inappropriate in view of our present modest objectives.

The area of agreement about *Hamlet* includes, one should suppose, the belief that it tells an absorbing story full of arresting episodes in magnificent language. Even a meaning, a basic meaning, will probably be agreed upon by most because the story treats of sin, suffering, and death, and the connection between the three seems not purely adventitious. Our difficulties have their origin actually in ourselves. In line with his usual practice, Shakespeare makes certain that we shall not view his play with passive acceptance, with the drowsy approval we vouchsafe a homily. By his usual method, he stimulates our moral natures until we see his tale of adventure and the wages of sin as a projection of all our sympathies and all our antipathies. Each composes a play as he reads and a new play on each successive reading. The method consists of offering us questions rather than statements, doubts rather than certainties, the heterogeneous rather than the homogeneous, an enigma rather than a demonstration. A multiple crime is reported by a multiple ghost to a multiple avenger.

First, let us consider the crime. In each of the earlier extant versions of the story (and it is vain to deal with the non-extant), there is a single clear version of the crime. In Saxo Grammaticus a man murders his brother, and is accepted in wedlock by his brother's widow although she is aware of his guilt.[25] In Belleforest, a man commits adultery with his brother's wife, then slays him, and weds the widow: the crime is 'double impiete, d'adultere incestueux, et de felonnie, et parricide.'[26] But what of Shakespeare's play? There are three possibilities in regard to the crime. In the Ghost's report it is the same crime as related in Belleforest. An 'adulterate beast' won to his lust the 'most seeming-virtuous' wife of his brother, dispatched him, and wedded her.[27] But is this what actually occurred? Claudius admits to fratricide but never to adultery.

> O, my offence is rank, it smells to heaven;
> It hath the primal eldest curse upon 't,
> A brother's murther![28]

Gertrude never admits to either adultery or knowledge of murder. She mentions her 'sin' or 'guilt' in general terms,[29] but it may consist only of an 'o'er hasty marriage'[30] to a brother-in-law—a marriage technically incestuous. The version of the crime presented in the mouse-trap playlet [31] is in line with Gertrude's own admissions rather than the Ghost's charges, and she herself never speaks or acts like an evil woman. Hamlet himself finally seems convinced that his mother has not committed adultery or connived at murder, although he is still filled with disgust at her sexual offense in marrying hastily in middle age an inferior man.[32] To inquire about the exact nature of a crime committed before the action of the play begins may seem like inquiring about the exact cause of the quarrel between the Montagues and the Capulets, but such is not the case. The sex motif in Hamlet is very prominent, and part of our excitement is caused by the curiosity and suspicion with which we always regard Gertrude.

There are then three defensible alternatives: that Claudius and Gertrude are murderers and adulterers, that they are murderers but not adulterers, that Claudius is a murderer but Gertrude nothing worse than an inconstant woman. If the last is the case, the Ghost either exaggerates or has, in the nether world, inferior sources of information. But this is a curious Ghost to begin with. It is really three ghosts. Santayana describes two: 'It is a Christian soul in Purgatory, which ought, in theological strictness, to be a holy and redeemed soul, a phase of penitential and spiritual experience; yet this soul fears to scent the morning air, trembles at the cock crow, and instigates the revenging of crime by crime.' [33] Its third identity is apparent when Hamlet can see it and his mother cannot, suggesting that it may be a mere hallucination. As Professor Campbell says, 'if a papist [who believed ghosts to be Christian spirits] and King James [who believed they were demons] and Timothy Bright [who believed they were figments of the brain] had seen the play, as they probably did, each would have gone home confirmed in his own opinion about ghosts.' [34] Shakespeare is said to have enacted this part himself—an appropriate role for one who has been pictured as divine spirit, sorcerer, and non-existent. There is no ghost in the extant earlier versions of the story, but one seems to have been introduced into it by the author of an earlier Hamlet play. If this author was Kyd, we should judge from the Andrea of his *Spanish Tragedy* that his ghost was a spirit only, and not, like Shakespeare's, a troubler of spirits.

An ambiguous ghost is an unreliable witness, and we have then the first but by no means the only element in Hamlet's dilemma. Hamlet, aside from the extension which each of us gives him, is what he says and does in the play. He is his dilemma. He is a multiple Hamlet because his is a multiple dilemma. Should he slay Claudius or not? And should he do so now or later? All the countless analyses of Hamlet's character are really attempts to answer the question: *Why does not Hamlet slay Claudius now?*

We may dismiss at once as the reason Shakespeare's compulsion to imitate the Ur-Hamlet, his inability to cope with intransigent material, or his nervousness lest prompt action in the Prince would leave him nothing to do with his last two acts. These explanations are psychologically interesting, representing the natural human impulse of analysts to transfer their bafflement to Shakespeare, but they have no other significance. A moment's reflection will determine that the element of compulsion is not a factor. Shakespeare was not forced to write this play or to treat its subject in any prescribed manner. The story was a legend with which he could deal as freely as with the legend of Timon of Athens. He could treat any earlier play upon it as he had treated *King Leir* or *Promos and Cassandra*. Hamlet could have slain Claudius in the second act, as Macbeth slew Duncan, without leaving the playwright at a loss. It would simply have meant that he had chosen to write a different play. But the irrefragable fact is that he chose to write *this* play, and the play as it is must be, at least approximately, the play as he wished it to be. The question, *Why does not Hamlet slay Claudius now?* is quite legitimate; and below are the proffered answers:

1

Hamlet is squeamish about blood. We are apt to dismiss this answer with disdain. Goethe's tender prince does not appeal to us; yet we must admit that in our own experience it is difficult enough drowning a litter of kittens, not to mention sticking knives into people. Our standards of endurance are very high—for people in plays.

2

Hamlet is ill. He is suffering from 'melancholy adust,' or the apathy of grief, or hysteria, or mere mental derangement, quite apart from his being 'fat and scant of breath.'

This answer is very much in favor in our present age of mental and medical clinics.

3

Hamlet must act with regard for his personal safety. This is never offered as the whole answer. The explanation is too uninteresting and, although the Prince does call himself a 'coward,' it has too little confirmation in the text. Significantly, however, it is practically the whole answer in Saxo Grammaticus and Belleforest.

4

Hamlet does not believe in the righteousness of personal vengeance. This, too, is an unpopular answer although it is the one favored by so distinguished a critic as Santayana.[35] It is rather amusing to observe how many civilized and Christian commentators, Coleridge for instance, have been able to give an easy nod of approval to lynch law, or at least to accept its righteousness in the ethical world of *Hamlet* as if the immorality of personal vengeance were an unfamiliar notion to Elizabethans. Few moral notions were unfamiliar to Elizabethans. A warning against vengeance, at least as directed at kings, appears in the Belleforest version of the Hamlet story itself,[36] and all moralists of the time fulminated against it. In rejecting it as an expressed motive for Hamlet's delay, Shakespeare is not revealing a moral blind spot.

5

Hamlet has an 'Oedipus complex' and unconsciously distrusts his own reasons for hating Claudius. This is a specialist's contribution, and we cannot greet it with enthusiasm. We must admit, however, that the Prince, in his conscious mind at least, is tremendously concerned about the sex-life of his mother.

6

Hamlet does not think that vengeance will serve any useful purpose. It will not restore his dead father or remove from him personally the soilure of having an adulterous, or at least a sensual, mother. This answer has not figured prominently in Shakespearean criticism, but it expresses a popular attitude toward punishment and could be calculated to suggest itself to some sectors of any audience.

7

Hamlet resents the call of duty. The role he is destined to play will separate him from his college companions forever, and from the soft arms of Ophelia:

> The time is out of joint. O cursed spite
> That ever I was born to set it right.[37]

8

Hamlet must find a way to slay Claudius without exposing the guilt of Gertrude.

9

Hamlet must make certain that the crown of Denmark shall pass to the right head.

10

Hamlet must secure the evidence that will make the justice of slaying Claudius apparent to the world.

There are so many answers, so many reasons for delay that would be cogent indeed if anyone of us were actually placed in Hamlet's position, that any elegant gestures of dismissal (there is really no problem: the facts as they appear fail to warrant all this ado) must, if taken seriously, be evaluated as the bravery of men not under fire. We have yet to list the two most widely accepted answers:

11

Hamlet has the philosophical cast of mind that inhibits practical action.

12

Hamlet must confirm the Ghost's accusations and then find an auspicious moment for his deed.

The first of these favored explanations is the one offered by Coleridge and accepted almost universally during the nineteenth century. It has the valuable endorsement of Hamlet himself—

> . . . I
> A dull and muddy-mettled rascal, peak
> Like John-a-dreams, unpregnant of my cause.[38]

And again—

> . . . the native hue of resolution
> Is sicklied o'er with the pale cast of thought,

And enterprises of great pith and moment
With this regard their currents turn awry
And lose the name of action.[39]

And again—

Sure he that made us with such large discourse
Looking before and after, gave us not
That capability and godlike reason
To fust in us unus'd. Now, whether it be
Bestial oblivion, or some craven scruple
Of thinking too precisely on th' event,—
A thought which, quarter'd, hath but one part wisdom
And ever three parts coward,—I do not know
Why yet I live to say 'This thing's to do,'
Since I have cause, and will, and strength, and means
To do't.[40]

To say that Coleridge had no reason for seeing in Hamlet's character the things he saw is absurd. They are there for all of us to see. But they are not the only things. Moreover, the whole philosophical implication of the reading seems somehow askew. It implies that Hamlet's bad example should spur us to action—any kind of action. We must think of him as culpable, rather than as baffled like ourselves, seeking truth, trying to piece together a puzzle with the essential parts missing. Tired of thought, Hamlet admires Fortinbras' meaningless action in invading Poland, prefers Fortinbras' type of futility to his own; and, tired of thought, Samuel Coleridge concurs, as in some part of our response most of us concur. But does existence offer only a choice between thought without action and action without thought? And if so, is the latter the better choice?

Must we assume that the mind is not as good as the stuff it has to work upon? The exaltation of action leads us to some rather somber reflections. Shakespeare spurred John Payne Collier to *action*—literary forgery. And *Hamlet* for a time was read as an indictment by old, unmilitaristic, philosophical Germany. In 1877, after the first of Germany's three modern descents upon France, Horace Howard Furness dedicated his New Variorum edition of *Hamlet*

To the

'GERMAN SHAKESPEARE SOCIETY'
of Weimar
Representative of a People
WHOSE RECENT HISTORY
has proved

ONCE FOR ALL

that

'GERMANY IS *NOT* HAMLET'

'True, true,' we must say,—'O would that it were not so!'

The second of the favored explanations of Hamlet's delay also finds much authority in the text. Hamlet cannot trust the statement of the Ghost, and is not sure that vengeance is in order until after the performance of the mouse-trap play in the third act. He fails to slay Claudius just afterwards because, as he explains, Claudius is at prayer. Then he is sent out of the country. Hamlet deals actively enough with Polonius behind the arras, and with Rosencrantz and Guildenstern at sea. It is all very reasonable: Hamlet is a man of action. There are only two difficulties with the reading: first, that it renders irrelevant most of the impressions we derive from the play, and second, that Hamlet never does end his delay to take deliberate action. Instead he performs in a fencing-match for Claudius, whom he finally slays almost as an inadvertence.

It is remarkable that the two most plausible single answers to *Why does not Hamlet slay Claudius now?* are mutually contradictory. Our conclusion must be that there is no single answer to the question. There are many answers, or rather many combinations of answers, with each member in each combination susceptible to innumerable degrees of emphasis. The possible range of variation of response is therefore unlimited. It is useless to debate the extent to which all this was a matter of conscious calculation with Shakespeare. No one knows what occurs within the creative mind. It is true that the play contains some purely accidental inconsistencies—on Hamlet's age for instance—and that some of its contradictory elements are traceable to anterior treatments of the story. Much of the old legend remains. Amleth or Amlethus is the folk hero of clever retorts and acute devices, and is harmoniously transfigured into the man of intellectual subtlety: foxiness becomes philosophical aptitude. Shakespeare retained whatever in the traditional story served his purpose, including the contradictions—which do not show as contradictions while we read. The amazing thing is that he could suggest so many explanations for Hamlet's conduct—that is for Hamlet—and commit himself to none of them. He has left this man, who is sad and gay, arrogant and humble, cruel and kind, brutal and tender, who can mock the aged but forbid others from doing so, who can talk bawdry but worship purity, who can kill, 'lug the guts into the neighbour room,' [42] and then 'weep for what is done' [43] as something for us to consider—an enduring moral enigma. It is the most astonishing balancing feat in literature, and the play provides more pleasurable excitement than any other in the world.

Chapter VII

THE UNRELIABLE SPOKESMAN

An academic building dear to this author through years of association contains Shakespearean mottoes upon the doors of its vestibule:

* * * *

Talkers are no good doers.

* * * *

Your If is the only peacemaker. Much
virtue in If.

* * * *

Self-love, my liege, is not so vile a sin
As self-neglecting.

* * * *

The architect must have been playful or unlucky. In its context the first of these utterances comes from a murderer about to go into action,[1] the second from a Clown praising cowardly evasion,[2] and the third from a braggart Frenchman.[3] The moral sentences most frequently quoted from the plays prove quite often to have emanated from a villain or a fool. The most common deliverances on *reputation*, that it is 'oft got without merit and lost without deserving'[4] and, conversely, that

. . . he that filches from me my good name
Robs me of that which not enriches him
And makes me poor indeed,—[5]

both come from hypocritical Iago, busy about his usual trade of blasting reputations. Such maxims, to be sure, are not nugatory simply because of their spokesmen: those about moderation in grief delivered by the evil Claudius in *Hamlet* [6] are repeated substantially by good Lafew in *All's Well that Ends Well*,[7] and the advice to a son by foolish Polonius [8] is echoed by the wise Countess of Rossillion.[9] Schlegel proposed that the 'sage maxims are not infrequently put in the mouth of stupidity, to show how easily such commonplace truisms may be acquired,' [10] but this does not explain why they are put into the mouth of villainy as well. It is dangerous to speak of Shakespeare's purposes, but we can safely speak of his effects. The effect, in this particular, is to throw the maxims a little out of focus, to blur them somewhat, to rob them of finality.

A similar effect is produced by the way in which moral maxims are received by the Shakespearean characters who hear them. Claudio on his way to prison says,

> As surfeit is the father of much fast
> So every scope by the immoderate use
> Turns to restraint. Our natures do pursue,
> Like rats that ravin down their proper bane,
> A thirsty evil, and when we drink we die.[11]

Lucio applauds, but then adds, 'I had as lief have the foppery of freedom as the morality of imprisonment.' If we say that Lucio is being portrayed as a cynic, what shall we say of Portia? Nerissa's identical piece of moralizing, 'they are as sick that surfeit with too much as they that starve with nothing,' draws from Portia the dry comment, 'Good sentences and well pronounc'd.' [12] The warm response of the stupid as well as the cold response of the intelligent sets sententiousness a'shimmering. An air of *performance* marks the long speech in which Friar Laurence disputes with Romeo of his estate. Not Romeo but the Nurse applauds—

> O Lord, I could have stay'd here all night
> To hear good counsel! O, what learning is! [13]

Shakespeare's characters are especially intolerant when the words of wisdom are offered in consolation. In *The Comedy of Errors* Luciana preaches meekness to the neglected wife Adriana, and Adriana replies:

> A wretched soul bruis'd with adversity
> We bid be quiet when we hear it cry;
> But were we burd'ned with like weight of pain
> As much, or more, we should ourselves complain.[14]

In *King Richard the Second*, Gaunt tells banished Bolingbroke that

> . . . gnarling sorrow hath less power to bite
> The man that mocks at it and sets it light.

But Bolingbroke replies,

> O, no! The apprehension of the good
> Gives but the greater feeling to the worse.
> Fell sorrow's tooth does never rankle more
> Than when he bites, but lanceth not the sore.[15]

The wise friar's offer of 'Adversity's sweet milk, philosophy' calls forth from Romeo,

> Hang up philosophy!
> Unless philosophy can make a Juliet.[16]

Poor Leonato of *Much Ado about Nothing* is especially explicit in his rejection of 'counsel'—

> Charm ache with air and agony with words.
> No, No! 'Tis all men's office to speak patience
> To those that wring under the load of sorrow,
> But no man's virtue nor sufficiency
> To be so moral when he shall endure
> The like himself . . .
> . . . I will be flesh and blood;
> For there was never yet philosopher
> That could endure the tooth ache patiently,
> However they have writ the style of gods
> And made a push at chance and sufferance.[17]

Then there is the agonized cry of Brabantio in Othello:

> But words are words. I never yet did hear
> That the bruis'd heart was pieced through the ear.[18]

To words of wisdom the response of suffering humanity in Shakespeare is 'No, No!' and the poet who is inimitable at framing moral maxims never portrays them as doing the slightest good.

Often in Shakespeare the moral evaluation of one character by another is provocative rather than accurate. Soon after Proteus has revealed himself to us as completely faithless, we hear Julia say,

> His words are bonds, his oaths are oracles
> His love sincere, his thoughts immaculate . . .
> His tears pure messengers sent from his heart,
> His heart as far from fraud as heaven from earth.[19]

Gratiano describes excellently the spurious pose of wisdom in the owl-like man,[20] but his words are quite misapplied to Antonio the Venetian merchant. Cornwall's eloquence is remarkable as he describes the affection of honest bluntness,[21] but his words have nothing to do with Kent at whom they are directed. The Countess of Rossillion praises Helena for the only good quality she really lacks—freedom from guile.[22] These false characterizations function in a curious way: they do not tell us what a character is like but make us question ourselves about him.

Many lengthy speeches in Shakespeare, full of moral philosophy, prove to be questions not statements when viewed in relation to the action. Friar Laurence preaches a sermon on eternal life as Capulet, Lady Capulet, County Paris, the Nurse, and others grieve at the bedside of Juliet:

> . . . Heaven and yourself
> Had part in this fair maid! now heaven hath all,
> And all the better is it for the maid . . .[23]

and so on. But of all those present only the speaker knows, as we in the audience know, that Juliet is not really dead. What are we to think of his laudation of death as eternal life? Brutus upbraids Cassius for taking money:

> . . . shall we now
> Contaminate our fingers with base bribes,
> And sell the mighty space of our large honours
> For so much trash as may be grasped thus?
> I had rather be a dog and bay the moon
> Than such a Roman.[24]

And again the action of the play throws a strange light on the sentiments expressed. Cassius has failed to send on 'certain sums of gold' which Brutus himself has demanded.

Shakespeare does not permit Cassius to ask if his accuser simply wants someone other than himself to perform the ugly task of wringing 'from the hard hand of peasants their vile trash,' [25] but the spectator can scarcely avoid asking the question. One of the most resounding speeches in Shakespeare,

> Time hath, my lord, a wallet at his back
> Wherein he puts alms for oblivion—[26]

figures in the play as the means by which wily Ulysses whets on Achilles to seek that very fame described as transitory. The speaker is insincere, the listener presumed to be gullible, and the spectator, therefore, tacitly invited to some independent reflection. When the contrast between the moralizing and the situation provoking it is obvious, the effect is comic, as in Petruchio's speech on 'the mind that makes the body rich' [27] while he is denying Kate a new suit of clothes. We have then something approaching the moral paradox previously discussed. The contrasts suggested here—and the reader may recall Portia's wonderful speech on mercy addressed to a man predestined to ignore it and to be used unmercifully—are less overt but equally impressive illustrations of moral stimulation without didactic intent.

Whenever in a play by Shakespeare there is a commentator on the worth of the other characters or the significance of the action, there is always something about him to prevent our relying too implicitly upon his words. This applies to such characters as Faulconbridge in *King John*, Berowne in *Love's Labour's Lost*, Jaques in *As You Like*

It, Lavatch in *All's Well that Ends Well,* Lucio in *Measure for Measure,* Apemantus in *Timon of Athens,* and Thersites in *Troilus and Cressida.* Each of these characters has been identified at various times as Shakespeare in disguise. But they are all eccentrics with satirical tongues; their fellow characters warn us against some of them, and against satire. The Duke addresses Jaques:

> Most mischievous foul sin, in chiding sin.
> For thou thyself hast been a libertine,
> As sensual as the brutish sting itself;
> And all th' embossed sores and headed evils
> That thou with license of free foot hast caught,
> Wouldst thou disgorge into the general world.[28]

The sycophantic poet in *Timon of Athens* projects a satire against flattery, and Timon asks, 'Wilt thou whip thine own faults in other men?'[29] In one play only by Shakespeare, *Troilus and Cressida,* does a spirit of mockery seem to prevail, and here if anywhere we might look for a satirist as Shakespeare's expositor. But Thersites is contemptibly base. We must agree with Coleridge that he is a 'devilish clever fellow'[30] but also with Professor Campbell that 'His voice is not the voice of Shakespeare. The spectators as well as all the characters in the play realize that his opinions are worthless. . . .'[31] Thersites is ridiculous, mulish, loathsome. If Shakespeare introduced himself into the play in this form, his mood must have been less sardonic than masochistic. As a matter of fact, Thersites does not so much expound *Troilus and Cressida* as epitomize it; he, like the play, demonstrates in his graceless character the inefficaciousness of ideals of conduct. It is the old story: we must attend to the character rather than to his opinions alone.

Characters serving as 'chorus' do actually appear but in much less conspicuous roles than those of Thersites and his fellow carpers. There are the two 'Lords' [32] in *All's Well that Ends Well,* the two 'Officers' [33] in *Coriolanus,* the three 'Strangers' [34] in *Timon of Athens,* the three 'Citizens' [35] in *King Richard the Third* and the anonymous 'Gentlemen' in this play and that. They are unassuming people who limit their remarks to a few fundamentals. Then there are, of course, the many minor characters who do little generalizing but are always ready to offer a word of sympathy or a helping hand. These, too, are a kind of 'chorus,' telling us that the earth still spins quietly on its axis. If Shakespeare had introduced into a play a man of good will, sane and judicious, who explained his fellow characters—if Horatio, let us say, had expounded Hamlet—we might conclude that Shakespeare was speaking and let it go at that. But such never occurs. Evidently the dramatist did not wish to be so helpful, did not wish to let us remain so passively acceptive. Perhaps he would have considered such an offering less a play than an animated lecture. At any rate, his critical commentators like Jaques and Thersites are suspicious items.

The three speeches in Shakespeare most commonly quoted in our own chaotic times as expressing the poet's personal convictions are those on order and degree by the Archbishop of Canterbury [36] in *King Henry the Fifth,* by Ulysses [37] in *Troilus and Cressida,* and by Menenius [38] in

Coriolanus. One is inclined to agree that Shakespeare, since few people favor chaos, believed in the main purport of these speeches. We may set this down to coincidence. That he was pausing at these three moments to inculcate principles, that he was moralizing rather than providing moral interest, is another matter. Perhaps one can be too fastidious in requiring disinterestedness of one's philosophers, but it cannot be ignored that each of the three speeches is delivered by an unscrupulous politician meeting an immediate problem—advocating a practical program of somewhat debatable merit.

Certain words common in Shakespearean criticism have been avoided in the foregoing discussion: *indifference, impartiality, irony.* They are imperfectly descriptive because all imply an attitude on the part of the dramatist incompatible with the effects he produces. These plays are not *ironical* except in the sense that all art is ironical in seeming to be the thing it is not. They do not belittle or mock life or our moral values; instead they are immensely cognizant of the importance of both. They are not *impartial* in the sense that their creator seemed to fear he might induce us to make improper decisions on debatable issues; Shakespeare is not functioning as a referee. *Indifference,* too, or objectivity, has the wrong connotation—of coldness, skepticism, even slackness. The word *accommodating* would be preferable to any of them were it not for the ignobility of its suggestions. The best word of all, obvious but inevitable, is simply *artistic.* These plays are deft. We are the instruments, and Shakespeare knows our stops.

PART TWO

Pleasurable Reassurance

CHAPTER I

JUSTICE IN COMIC FABLE

It is one thing to be stimulated and another to be disturbed. The too-earnest or too-awkward practitioner who cannot massage the skin without rubbing it off, or knead the muscles without breaking the bones, will not build up a great clientele. If *King Lear* had meant to its audience what it is sometimes said to mean, there would have been panic at the Globe. The people there—the felmonger from Southwark, the clerk from St. Marie Wolmers, the carrier's daughter from Holborn, the pewterer's wife from Lothbury, the shopkeepers, students, courtiers, and servants—did not want to hear that life is a tale told by an idiot or that clouds of glory trail in the Boar's Head Inn. They were not prepared for a two-hour operation in which old principles were cut away and new ones grafted in. They were too frugal to sacrifice to the day's entertainment the truths they lived by, and accept in exchange sheer loneliness and fear.

We must consider, then, those qualities in Shakespeare that are reassuring, that let the spectator retain his inner tranquillity, that, despite all the surface flux and agitation, provide something stable and fixed. It has been remarked earlier that Shakespeare makes us wonder whether Falstaff is a coward but not whether cowardice is a vice. That cowardice is a vice may, like any other moral certainty, be paradoxically denied, but it remains a certainty. The principle is not argued but taken for granted: it is a Shakespearean postulate. The idea that cowardice is a vice is not subtle, but it is the only kind of idea that the plays indubitably endorse. It is worthwhile considering these ideas; to refined intellects they are apt to prove confusingly simple.

The earliest book about Shakespeare's morality consists of sententious passages quoted, with commentary, from one play after another in the manner of earlier compilations extolling his 'beauties.' The estimable Mrs. Griffith seems to have planned originally to supply also the moral of each play as a whole, and she does so with the first. *The Tempest* teaches—

That the ways, the justice, and the goodness of Providence, are so frequently manifested toward mankind, even in this life, that it should ever encourage an honest and a guiltless mind to form hopes, in the most forlorn situations; and ought also to warn the wicked never to rest assured in the false confidence of wealth or power, against the natural abhorrence of vice, both in God and man.[1]

But the next play in order was *A Midsummer Night's Dream*, and she was compelled to say, 'I shall not trouble my readers with the Fable of this piece, as I can see no general moral that can be deducted from the Argument,'[2] and of the next, *The Two Gentlemen of Verona*, she says, 'The Fable of this play has no more moral in it, than the former.'[3] With the fourth play, *Measure for Measure*, her tone becomes plaintive, 'I cannot see what moral can be extracted from this Piece,' [4] and with the fifth she throws in her hand: 'I shall take no further notice of the want of a moral fable in the rest of these plays.' [5]

It was the compiler's misfortune to begin with the comedies. Mrs. Griffith's powers of abstraction were not great, but she is not the last one who has had trouble deducing a moral from Shakespeare's comedies. The tragedies presumably are a different matter, and the notion is fairly prevalent that the tragedies convey a message whereas the comedies simply entertain. But such cannot be the case. Both species were presented to the same audience in the same place for the same purpose. On some days Shakespeare entertained with comedy, and on some days he entertained with tragedy or history. Anything so conspicuous as a scheme of justice cannot be applicable on one occasion and not on another, and there cannot be equity in the condemnation of a hypocrite like Iago unless there is also equity in the pardon of a hypocrite like Angelo, unless there are features that distinguish the offense of the latter from the offense of the former. It is not only that *Othello* would convey a 'moral' message and *Measure for Measure* an 'unmoral' one, but the very existence of *Measure for Measure* would cast suspicion upon the sincerity of *Othello*. Putting it another way, the moral nature of the audience is not reversible and must be satisfied equally by comedy and tragedy. The moral nature may be more deeply affected by tragedy, but not presumed to exist only when tragedy is billed. What follows is an attempt to show that there is a scheme of moral justice in Shakespeare's stories that is popularly satisfying, and that it not only applies equally to tragedy and comedy but accounts for the difference between the two.

We must begin with an examination of the idea of *poetical justice*. Aristotle's remark that a tragic hero without flaw would arouse in us not pity and fear, but horror, seems really to imply that, for the comfort of the spectator, disaster must be shown to be, in a measure at least, avoidable. Since Aristotle also insists that tragedy in general is concerned with men better than ourselves, he can scarcely be describing spectacles of personal retribution. The protagonist's flaw is a technical necessity, not justifying his suffering but indicating how he came to be exposed to suffering. The words of the philosopher have been given a moralistic turn that was never intended. The term 'poetical justice' was coined by Thomas Rymer [6] in the late seventeenth century, but the idea behind it had been a commonplace in neo-classical criticism for generations. The Aristotelian dictum is distorted to mean that, in any satisfying fable, vice must be shown to be punished and virtue to be rewarded.

The doctrine of poetical justice stands in the anomalous position of having been strengthened by those who have attacked it and weakened by those who have defended it. Two major charges have been leveled against the doctrine. The first rests upon an assumption that proves upon scrutiny to be inapplicable in the world of art. It implies that the facts of life and the facts of art must be identical, that art must be literally 'true to life.' The charge is interestingly worded by Joseph Addison in *The Spectator*: 'We find that Good and Evil happen alike to all Men on this Side the Grave.' Addison, let us notice, is echoing the scepticism and pessimism of Ecclesiastes: *the race is not to the swift, nor the battle to the strong . . . but time and chance happeneth to them all.* We must notice further that Addison does not push his point to its logical conclusion. He says that:

. . . the ancient Writers of Tragedy [including Shakespeare] treated Men in their Plays, as they are dealt with in the World, by making Virtue sometimes happy and sometimes miserable, as they found it in the Fable which they made choice of, or as it might affect their Audience in the most agreeable Manner.[7]

But he does not account for their failure to treat vice in the same way, or mention Aristotle's specific warning against their doing so. Presumably, if what happens in life is to be the arbiter, a certain number of plays should end with cheats and hypocrites pictured in tranquil possession of their ill-gotten gains.

The second charge against the doctrine of poetical justice is based upon transcendental ideals of morality. Professor Mortimer Adler becomes quite heated upon the subject:

No more immoral lesson could be taught. The doctrine of poetic justice is the teaching of Satan and the friends of Job. If there is a basic insight which both Greek and Christian share, it is that virtue is a condition of happiness and not of material success.[8]

But we must notice that lurking in the background of both Greek and Christian insight is the idea of a heaven and a hell. Happiness has its material aspects even in philosophy, and the dramatist is limited in his materials to the here and now. He must, if he is going to portray the virtuous as happy, employ concrete tokens; he cannot picture them simply as wearing beatific smiles, although some such idea seems to govern certain of the remarks of Bradley upon *King Lear*.[9] To deny, with however much moral fervor, that in general the product of virtue is well-being, is to render it no service, but to blur the distinction between virtue and vice.

John Dennis is said to have grown so wrothy about Addison's estimate of poetical justice that, in Lintot's bookshop, he ripped Number Forty from a volume of *The Spectator* and threw it in the street.[10] In a relatively unfrenzied mood, Dennis actually supplies the answers to the objections of both an Addison and an Adler. As to good and evil happening alike to all men in life, he says it is both a false and a dangerous assertion, for 'we neither know what Men really are, nor what they really suffer,'[11] and as to the portrayal of material rewards and punishments, he says that the poet is 'forc'd by temporal to represent eternal Punishments'[12]—in a word, to use symbols. But Dennis's argument also reveals the defect in the doctrine of poetical justice as commonly applied. When the virtuous are pictured as suffering, we must conclude that they are not truly virtuous or that the dramatist has written a faulty play. Dennis is at least clear-sighted enough to choose the latter alternative, and he instances the fate of such characters as Duncan, Cordelia, and Lady Macduff as the dramatist's 'errors.'[13] Others, less clear-sighted although more devoted to Shakespeare, have chosen the first alternative and discovered in Shakespeare's virtuous sufferers tragic 'flaws.' The flaws, to be sure, are sometimes present but not for the reasons these apologists maintain.[14]

That a character must be shown as morally culpable before he may be shown as suffering is absurd on the face of it. Tragedy ceases to be tragedy and becomes a juridical display. Cordelia is not murdered but executed, and the villains are not villains but agents of justice. And what justice it is! For flaws so slight that they escape the average eye, the whole fabric is torn to pieces. It is difficult to imagine how any assembly of human beings could mistake such a travesty for justice, and could go away pleased and satisfied. Shakespeare never for a moment suggests that there is an element of retribution for personal faults in the fates of character like Cordelia, Duncan, and Lady Macduff. His portrayal of cause and effect is of an entirely different nature, and infinitely more satisfying. It applies in both tragedy and comedy, and conforms more nearly to the idea of Aristotle than to the ideas of those who have interpreted Aristotle or of those who have attacked the interpreters. What Shakespeare does is to remove the onus from agents and place it on the thing itself: he does not punish evil persons and reward virtuous ones, but condemns evil and praises virtue by portraying their contrasted effects.

Before dealing further with the matter, we must attempt a classification of Shakespeare's stories. They fall into two major divisions: fables, and histories. The fables include all those plays commonly called comedies or romances and most of those plays commonly called tragedies. The distinguishing mark of the fables is that, to whatever extent some of their events may be considered to have actually happened in the more or less remote past, those events have no final authority in determining the dramatist's version of them. He is free, or relatively free, to alter and invent. In the extant versions of the fable preceding Shakespeare's, Hamlet has quite an extensive career after he slays his uncle. The fact that a Timon or a Titus Andronicus once actually lived, as did a Macduff and possibly a Lear, does not alter the fact that their stories are fables. In these fables the relationship among the characters is mainly personal and domestic, not political; and vice and virtue operate on individuals directly, not through the intermediary of national programs or party platforms. The histories, on the other hand, include the ten English chronicle plays, and also *Julius Caesar, Antony and Cleopatra, Coriolanus* and *Troilus and Cressida*. Although the story of Troilus was actually as fabulous as the story of Lear, it was not so conceived. Shakespeare could alter the one to let Lear die, but he could not alter the other to let Hector live. He could ward off a conquest of ancient Britain, but he could not ward off a conquest of ancient Troy. He was in *Troilus and Cressida* dealing, in effect, with history. In addition to limiting his freedom of treatment, the stories of history present the dramatist with conflicts between factions and nations as a determining factor. In *King Lear*, France fights Britain for personal reasons; in *Troilus and Cressida*, Hector fights Achilles for national reasons. The relationship between characters is not purely personal and domestic, and the moral choices of each are often determined for him by his cause.

Dealing first with the fables as distinct from the histories, we notice that although some are gayer than others, it would be difficult to distinguish among them on this basis. There is no gaiety in *Cymbeline* but a great deal in *Hamlet*, yet the latter belongs properly with cheerless *Macbeth*, the former properly with cheerful *Twelfth Night*. The distinction between the fables is this—that some of them end in marriages and some of them end in death, or, to put it less distractingly, in some of the fables the major characters proceed to happiness and in others they proceed to sorrow. In the former there may be an occasional unregenerate character like Shylock left in trouble, and in the latter an occasional lucky one like Fortinbras left with occasion for secret rejoicing, but the contrast is clear on the whole. In some plays the good and the bad alike are left pretty well off, and in others the good and bad alike must be prepared for burial.

There are seventeen fables that end happily, and although we call them comedies or romances, we must observe that the plot elements which compose them are identical with the plot elements of the tragedies. The course of human life is troubled by chance, by villainy, and by unbridled passions. There is unfounded suspicion of adultery in *The Merry Wives of Windsor* and *The Winter's Tale* as well as in *Othello*, usurpation and inordinate ambition in *As You Like It* and *The Tempest* as well as in *Macbeth*, ill-disposed parents in *A Midsummer Night's Dream* and *The Two Gentlemen of Verona* as well as in *Romeo and Juliet.* Don John of *Much Ado about Nothing* and Iachimo of *Cymbeline* traduce a pure woman as does Iago of *Othello.* Proteus projects a rape,[15] Oliver a murder,[16] and Angelo the equivalent of both. In fact we are presented by these comedies with some remarkably murderous specimens: Leontes orders the murder of his baby daughter,[17] Posthumus the murder of his wife,[18] and Antonio and Sebastian undertake in person the murder of their sovereign lord.[19] Shylock as well as Lear has reason to know how 'sharper than a serpent's tooth it is to have a thankless child.' Their story material makes most of these comedies potential tragedies.

If tragedy seems just because erring mortals pay the penalty for their errors, what can we say of these comedies where erring mortals pay no penalty but actually receive rewards? The form that the reflection usually takes is that Proteus does not *deserve* Julia, or Claudio Hero, or Bertram Helena, or Lysimachus Marina; and certainly Angelo does not *deserve* Mariana or anything else except the whipping-post. Let us make a test case of this last and most notable instance, in these plays of Shakespeare destined to end happily, of the dramatist's presumed offense against our sense of justice by failing to punish vice. Coleridge says, 'cruelty with lust and damnable baseness, cannot be forgiven, because we cannot conceive them as being morally repented of'[20] and 'our feelings of justice are grossly wounded in Angelo's escape.'[21] Although Angelo's escape has never been subject for rejoicing, some critics have been more charitable. The play, says Pater, deals with 'the difficulty of just judgment' and suggests that 'true justice is in its essence a finer knowledge through love.'[22] The most common comment is that the play has a patched-up ending, but this apology has the defect of that which attributes the inconsistencies in *Hamlet* to the influence of its non-extant predecessor. Shakespeare was not compelled to write *Measure for Measure,* or to end it in any particular way. The inference is that the play with its present ending must have been in his mind a single and satisfying conception. Lawrence says, 'The ending of the play, then, really contradicts the title,' but apologizes, 'The claims of strict justice are secondary to those of stage entertainment.'[23] It is a question, however, whether an audience can both be entertained and have its sense of justice grossly wounded.

As a matter of fact, the ending of *Measure for Measure* does not contradict the title but exactly illustrates it, and illustrates also the conception of justice that prevails in all these plays of Shakespeare, with tragic potentialities and untragic endings. Duke Vincentio says,

> For this new-married man approaching here,
> Whose salt imagination yet hath wrong'd
> Your well-defended honour, you must pardon
> For Mariana's sake. But as he adjudg'd your brother—
> Being criminal in double violation
> Of sacred chastity, and of promise-breach
> Thereon dependent for your brother's life—
> The very mercy of the law cries out
> Most audible, even from his proper tongue,
> 'An Angelo for Claudio! death for death!'
> Haste still pays haste, and leisure answers leisure,
> Like doth quit like, and Measure still for Measure.

The reply is spoken by Isabella and anticipates the moment when Claudio will be proved alive so that the sentence of 'death for death' can no longer apply:

> His act did not o'ertake his bad intent,
> And must be buried but as an intent
> That perish'd by the way. Thoughts are no subjects,
> Intents but merely thoughts.[24]

These words cannot be dismissed as a quibble. They express the sum of human experience in matters pertaining to punishment—the wisdom underlying the administration of justice in all civilized communities. To follow an unaccomplished murder by an accomplished execution is not measure for measure. A man who fires at another man but misses his mark is found guilty of a high misdemeanor but not sent to the gallows. A man fully equipped with mask, dark-lantern, and tools found lurking beside a rear window is not judged guilty of burglary. No one is a murderer until he has murdered, and no one is a burglar until he has forcibly entered. We may justifiably suspect that a last-second change of mind is a less likely explanation than poor markmanship for the unaccomplished murder, but we cannot be sure. We may doubt that our trespasser was there in the shadows in order to bury his burglar tools, and may wonder about his future, but we can deal only with the facts at hand. Practical justice dare not proceed on the speculation of future evil; and frustrated intentions lie outside its jurisdiction. 'The devil himself,' said Brian in 1478, 'knoweth not the mind of man.' The law has become increasingly interested in the *mens rea*, but chiefly as a means of determining the extent to which the rigor of punishment for accomplished crimes should be mitigated. The possession *per se* of a guilty mind is not punishable.[25]

Isabella herself profits, although not to the extent of Angelo, by the distinction that must be made between intentions and accomplished deeds. Let us presume that the story had ended as follows: Isabella after refusing the plea of her frightened brother that she sacrifice her chastity to save his life, and after giving him the tongue-lashing she does in the play as it stands, returns to the nunnery of St. Clare, still 'a thing enskied and sainted.'[26] We then see Claudio, still contrite after her humiliating rebuke, go humbly to his death. Would Isabella still be the heroine of the play? In the earlier versions of the story by the Giraldis, and by Whetstone, the woman yields to the corrupt deputy and then is 'rehabilitated' by marriage to him. Shakespeare rejected this marriage and this yielding. He rejected also the alternative of letting her yield and then take her own life, an acceptable pattern of conduct for tragedy. No one would have condemned her choice, or believed that thus to redeem her brother with her body meant that her soul must 'die forever.'[27] Isabella's position in the play is morally precarious. Her initial course in striving to save her brother's life instead of ministering to his spirit she enters reluctantly, evidently aware of its defect; and it is her own palliation of her brother's sin of fornication—one that 'many have committed' . . . a 'natural guiltiness'[28]—that helps stir the lust of Angelo. The scene[29] in which Angelo makes his proposal and Isabella replies is one of the most fascinating in Shakespeare because here if anywhere we can see the puppet-master's hand. The scale is tipped constantly in her favor during the debate, not only because of the tremendously high value placed upon chastity in these plays, but because Isabella's decision is justified only in the light of subsequent accidents.

Putting it briefly then, in Shakespeare's plays as in our courts, offenders are punished in the degree that their offenses have taken effect. It has been said by Brandes that his are the 'ethics of intention,' [30] meaning that his people are judged by what they intend rather than by what they do. The opposite is more nearly the case. On one occasion Angelo is asked if he might not in his youth, opportunity and inclination conspiring, have committed Claudio's offense, to which he replies,

> 'Tis one thing to be tempted, Escalus,
> Another thing to fall.[31]

And in Shakespeare it is a third thing—and the only punishable one—to succeed. Characters are punished not for what they intend, or what they attempt, but for what they accomplish. If this is too pragmatic a scheme of justice to please delicate tastes, it can only be said that the plays themselves constantly concede its limitations and express as a commonplace the thought that mankind is lucky—that if those sins were punished which are open to the sight of God, none of us should 'scape whipping.' [32] Let us trust that those who thirst for the blood of Angelo are in a sound position to prefer this less practical type of justice.

When mere exposure of the frustrated malefactor might seem insufficient, Shakespeare was inclined to mete out 'token' punishment or else to defer the painful business until some time after the action of the play had ceased. Caliban, Trinculo, and Stephano can expiate the offense of attempted murder by decorating Prospero's cell! [33] The treatment of the three blackguards in *Much Ado about Nothing* is typical. We do not learn what, if anything, is to happen to Conrade and Borachio, and as for Don John, we must trust that Benedick will interrupt his honeymoon to attend to the matter:

Think not on him till to-morrow. I'll devise thee brave punishments for him. Strike up, pipers! *Dance.*[34]

The epilogue to *Pericles* gives more attention than is usual to rewards and punishments, but nevertheless it contrasts strikingly with the analogous matter in Laurence Twine's *Patterne of Painefull Aduentures*. In Twine the bawd (who has operated with the Governor's connivance) is burnt, although the Governor himself is permitted to wed the royal virgin whom the bawd had vainly tried to exploit. The pander, for getting the virgin honest work (after vainly assailing her himself), is rewarded with 200 pieces of gold. The other inmates of the brothel are provided independent means for life. The treatment of the pirates who abducted the virgin is especially arresting:

And for that he knew that the sinister means which they hitherto had usued was caused most by constraint, for want of other trade or abilitie to live by, he therefore made them all knights, and gave them plenty of gold and silver, and indowed them also with great possessions.[35]

For these stirrings of social conscience we must give Twine credit, at the same time admitting some inner dissatisfaction. Unless the author consults the reader, or includes in his tale a competent jury, it is unwise to indicate who shall be knighted and who shall be burnt. Shakespeare was both more just than Twine and more artistically canny.

The fables ending happily require of sinners one other thing besides ineffectuality before lightly dismissing them, and that is penitence—or rather a token portion of the full schedule of open confession, repentance of sins, and amendment of life. Valentine says of the expeditious repentance of Proteus,

> Who by repentance is not satisfied
> Is nor of heaven nor earth; for these are pleas'd;
> By penitence th' Eternal wrath's appeas'd.[36]

A moment later we hear that even the band of outlaws

> . . . are reformed, civil, full of good,
> And fit for great employment.[37]

Except in *All's Well that Ends Well*, where Bertram's act of contrition is composed of a single word and some dumb-show (though it suffices to make Lafew weep),[38] this is the quickest work in the plays, but in none of them is the business long drawn out. In *As You Like It*, Oliver repents in our presence,[39] but Duke Frederick meets the obligation offstage,

> . . . meeting with an old religious man,
> After some question with him, was converted
> Both from his enterprise and from the world.[40]

In Lodge's *Rosalynde*, he fails to meet this old religious man and has to be slain. Upon the sinners in *The Tempest* is urged

> . . . heart's sorrow
> And a clear life ensuing,[41]

and shortly later, we hear

> All three of them are desperate. Their great guilt
> Like poison given to work a great time after,
> Now 'gins to bite the spirits.[42]

Although there is still some doubt about Sebastian and Antonio, the end of the play takes Alonso's redemption for granted; and the last we hear from Caliban is his resolution to 'seek for grace.' [43] All things considered, Angelo's four lines in *Measure for Measure*—the last he speaks—are a creditable performance:

> I am sorry that such sorrow I procure;
> And so deep strikes it in my penitent heart
> That I crave death more willingly than mercy,
> 'Tis my deserving, and I do entreat it.[44]

It should be understood that the almost comic brevity of these acts of repentance does not diminish their importance. Shakespeare places a high value upon human dignity and does not consider scenes of humiliation pleasurable. In only one instance in the plays is a penitent nagged, and this, significantly, is an unchaste woman. Vincentio returns to his attack upon poor Julietta and forces from her the words,

> I do repent me as it is an evil
> And take the shame with joy.[45]

More of this would be too much. To complain of the suddenness and brevity of the scenes of repentance is to indict an artistic convention, not a scheme of justice. We may with equal logic condemn the use of disguise. In *The Two Gentlemen of Verona*, 'Sebastian' takes off a cap and becomes Julia again; her lover puts on penitence and becomes Proteus again. If anyone had told Shakespeare that he wished the scenes of repentance to be harder on the sinners and more convincing to himself—that he yearned for a full-dress display in sackcloth and ashes— the dramatist would probably have replied that the person showed curious taste in entertainment.

We may say that we should not care to have an Angelo, a Proteus, or a Bertram for a son-in-law. That is a salutary reflection, but somewhat immaterial. Mariana, Julia, and Helen want them for husbands, and if that is folly, it carries its own punishment with it. The married life of these couples lies outside the play, and we are free to be optimistic. One observer draws comfort in the case of Bertram from the fact that something can be hoped for on genetic grounds from one who had such excellent parents.[46] It is true that the defects of an Angelo or a Bertram may stand so conspicuously in the foreground that they obscure the design of the story. In the usual comedy we are less impressed with the moral defects of the character. Solinus in *The Comedy of Errors* is a Duke who personally accompanies to the place of execution a poor unfortunate who cannot meet certain financial requirements. He claims that he lacks power to qualify the law, although, as a matter of fact, he ignores the law in the end. We do not think of him as a merciless tyrant, both because Aegeon's head is never destined to fall and because no emphasis is placed upon the initial refusal of mercy. Solinus is a better example than Angelo of Shakespeare's methods in comedy. As a rule, in these fables destined to end well, the episodes are treated in a tone befitting the facts as they appear to the audience rather than as they appear to the characters in the play: Master Ford's soliloquy [47] when he thinks he is to be cuckolded does not express the anguish which Shakespeare would give a character actually in such danger; Claudio is fairly light-hearted after Hero's supposed demise; [48] and a character like Isabella would never part so casually from her stricken brother were he really destined to die.[49] Sometimes in the romances, and even elsewhere, the 'provisional' passions are given a true tragic intensity— the jealousy of Leontes for instance [50]—and we may justly question the artistry of the *genre*. What we really mean is that we cannot go so far as Shakespeare's original audience in accepting certain conventions. We are questioning a technique rather than a scheme of justice.

It should be observed that although there is a reluctance to punish sinners, there is an equal reluctance to

explain their sins away. The irreclaimable sinners are apt
to be marked by physical stigmata. Adriana's conception
of the worst possible combination of traits is significant:

> He is deform'd, crooked, old, and sere,
> Ill-fac'd, worse bodied, shapeless everywhere;
> Vicious, ungentle, foolish, blunt, unkind,
> Stigmatical in making, worse in mind.[51]

We may oppose to this the speech of Antonio in *Twelfth
Night:*

> In nature there's no blemish but the mind;
> None can be call'd deform'd but the unkind.
> Virtue is beauty; but the beauteous evil
> Are empty trunks o'erflourish'd by the devil.[52]

But it is worth observing that Antonio is led to this reflection by an error: the person to whom he refers is in truth
virtuous as well as beautiful. Shakespeare is disinclined to
endow the vicious with physical beauty. There are ancient
sanctions behind Oberon's incantation against birth-marks
on the children that will bless the marriages of *A Midsummer Night's Dream;* [53] and something archaic and, to
modern minds, possibly offensive attends Shakespeare's
assumption that ugliness or departure from the external
norm accompanies congenital vice or departure from the
internal norm. Swart Aaron says,

> Let fools do good, and fair men call for grace,
> Aaron will have his soul black as his face.[54]

And hunch-backed Richard says,

And this word 'love,' which greybeards call divine,
Be resident in men like one another,
And not in me! [55]

Bastardy, in Don John, Edmund, Orleans, and others carries with it a presumption of separation from normal men and their virtues. Jewishness also suggests moral alienation.[56] There are no hard and fast rules in the matter, and Shakespeare can portray a Jewess like Jessica, a Moor like Othello, and a bastard like Faulconbridge, without this presumption of moral abnormality; yet his tendency is in the opposite direction. Vice is something absolute, rooted irremovably in some individuals and lodged temporarily in others; it is not a mere natural effect of a natural cause. The fact that a sinful deed may result from poverty, ignorance, or misplaced zeal does not excuse it. Taunted with his share in slaying Prince Edward, Clarence in *King Richard the Third* does not attribute his act simply to devotion to his brother as he might well have done, but describes his 'motives' as, 'My brother's love, the devil, and my rage.' [57] That Dionyza of *Pericles* persecutes Marina because of devotion to her own daughter does not diminish her offense. That Saunder Simpcox and his wife of *King Henry the Sixth* can plead poverty does not save them from a beating for attempting to defraud.[58] In *Romeo and Juliet* the cruel wretchedness of the Apothecary is vividly pictured, but this seller of poison is addressed nevertheless in tones of bitter contempt. To 'motivate' a misdeed thoroughly is to excuse it, and much modern literature impales itself upon this dilemma. It motivates sin until its outlines are blurred. It seems hopeless for us to combat anything so natural, so inevitable; and we become indeed somewhat dissatisfied with our virtues. The Shakespearean method is less rational, but safer and more comforting: Sin is Sin, not excusable but pardonable—provided no second person has been irreparably injured.

If anything, Shakespeare errs on the side of severity. No one can cite an instance of an irreparable injury that is forgiven in these plays—mere physical inconvenience and mental anguish being sufficiently atoned by the presumed equivalent distress on the part of the exposed malefactor,—but there are, on the other hand, some merely intended injuries that are punished. Cloten in *Cymbeline* and a few other characters in the romances are actually slain. The most interesting case is that of Shylock. Professor Stoll, arguing Shakespeare's unsympathetic conception of the character, points out that Shylock receives the heaviest penalty to be found in the pound of flesh stories.[59] If Iachimo of *Cymbeline* can be pardoned, and if Falstaff of *Merry Wives of Windsor* can be invited to the concluding feast after a little pinching, why should Shylock be so hardly used? Antonio has actually lost neither his life nor his money. Would it not be appropriate for Shylock to repent, to bless his daughter and her husband as do other balked fathers in the comedies, and then be invited to a feast? The trouble seems to be that Shylock was in no position to accept the invitation:

I will buy with you, sell with you, talk with you, walk with you, and so following; but I will not eat with you, drink with you, nor pray with you.[60]

Shylock can violate his principles on occasion by eating with the Christians, but the fact remains that something other than his wicked past prevents reconciliation in this play. Shylock is a Jew. Christianity may be forced upon him, and he may express himself as 'content'—but he retains his isolation. Shakespeare, we may say, was anti-Semitic. On the other hand, to make Shylock repent, confer blessings, and accept the forgiving patronage of his enemies would imply a type of conversion perhaps more humiliating to him and to his race.

The happy endings of the comedies and romances, then, are the result of the triumph of virtue over vice. The vice may be a slight thing capable of the lightest treatment: the presumption of the young men of Navarre in *Love's Labour's Lost*, the shrewishness of Katherine in *The Taming of the Shrew*; it may be a disorder of the passions: the fickleness of Proteus in *The Two Gentlemen of Verona*, the self-conceit of Bertram in *All's Well that Ends Well*, the lust of Angelo in *Measure for Measure*, the jealousy of Leontes in *The Winter's Tale*; it may be villainy: that of malicious Shylock in *The Merchant of Venice*, envious Don John in *Much Ado about Nothing*, covetous Oliver and Duke Frederick in *As You Like It*, treacherous Thaliard and Dionyza in *Pericles*, the evil Queen and Cloten besides Iachimo in *Cymbeline*, the ruthlessly ambitious lords of *The Tempest*. Mere circumstances may form an obstacle to happiness, but it is rarely the only one. In addition to the confusion of identities and the farcical misadventures in *The Comedy of Errors*, there is the jealousy of Adriana:

> The venom clamours of a jealous woman
> Poisons more deadly than a mad dog's tooth.[61]

Adriana must be *cured*, and this motif in the play represents a Shakespearean departure from Plautus. Usually there is not one but several moral obstacles in a single play, even the most farcical of them. In *The Merry Wives of Windsor*, there is the jealousy of Master Ford, the parental worldliness of Master Page, and the lecherousness of Sir John Falstaff. Parental intransigence is a common difficulty, appearing even in *A Midsummer Night's Dream*, where for the most part we must look for our moral defect among quarrelsome fairies. The ethical system of *The Two Noble Kinsmen* is that of a courtly cult, but if we accept, as we are expected to do, their tokens for realities, we witness the triumph of honor, courage, true love, and generosity.

The happiness that follows the elimination of evil, the triumph of good, consists in the Shakespearian world of reunion of kindred, the end of strife, and, above all, the mating of lovers. Shakespeare seems to have said of all his matings what Prospero says of Ferdinand and Miranda's:

> But this swift business
> I must uneasy make, lest too light winning
> Make the prize light.[62]

We must not miss the *moral satisfaction* conveyed by these matings. Our academic minds are apt to be a little dusty in this department, to be sicklied o'er with the pale cast of physiological or sociological rationalizing. That every Jack must have his Jill in a comedy we shrug off as a trifle. But clear eyes and unsullied spirits do not see the thing in this way. The union of a Ferdinand and Miranda, a Perdita and Florizel, a Rosalind and Orlando, a Fenton and sweet Anne Page, a Viola and Orsino, and all the rest—a Portia and Bassanio, Jessica and Lorenzo, even a Beatrice and Benedick, is a consummation devoutly to be wished. A couple, young, fair, faithful, pure, and ardently in love, win through to the type of fulfillment that everyone can understand: companionship of spirit and the pleasures of the 'long and well-deserved bed' [63]—the beginning of joyous increase. Life goes on to the lilt of flute and tabor. It is for good reason that the whole world loves a lover. Old men scent the spring, and my Bread Street housewife leaves the Globe with a contented smile rounding her ample cheeks. *The story has come out right.* We must not be too narrow in our view of what constitutes morality. Such marriages have a remarkably purifying effect; in fact it takes a good deal of antecedent criminality to set them off properly.

CHAPTER II

JUSTICE IN TRAGIC FABLE

In seventeen of Shakespeare's fables evil happily misses its mark. In seven others evil unhappily finds its mark. It is in connection with the latter that the question of poetical justice is more often raised, and we are asked not why Angelo lives but why Cordelia perishes. Cordelia is by no means the only one about whom the question might be asked. There is, for instance, Duncan:

> . . . this Duncan
> Hath borne his faculties so meek, hath been
> So clear in his great office, that his virtues
> Will plead like angels, trumpet-tongu'd against
> The deep damnation of his taking-off.[1]

Yet taken off he is, in spite of his virtues—virtues of Shakespeare's own invention, because in Holinshed this Scottish king is a 'faint-hearted milkesop . . . feeble and slouthfull.'[2] Dennis considered his fate an artistic error,[3] and apologists have sought flaws in his character. Significantly, however, they have done so less frequently than in the case of Cordelia—for the evident reason that Duncan's fate pains us less. It is paradoxical that the very pity one feels for Cordelia must set one busy maligning her character. She is too uncompromising—perhaps like Isabella a little too intent upon her own integrity; a few amiable lies from her at the outset would have forestalled disaster. She has the 'tragic flaw,' and her fate is just. This position, of course, either attributes to her a sort of prescience—she has read *King Lear* and knows in advance the unlucky consequences of her truthfulness,—or it condones punishment out of all proportion to the offense. It disregards our total experience of life, for we look about us in vain for her moral equal and ask why any deserves to escape if Cordelia deserves to suffer. But we are battling here with a strawman. No one really believes in her culpability. The alternate position is little more tenable—that Cordelia's fate is a violation of poetical justice and a defect in the play. This can mean only that the play displeases moral people—denied on prima facie evidence,—or that it contravenes morality by setting a bad example. It comforts the vicious and confirms them in their vice by showing the painful fate of virtue represented by Cordelia as a symbol. What a curious picture this conjures up! We see the audience of the Globe as two thousand gargoyles cackling with glee like witches at their sabbath. Of course, *King Lear* would be a comedy in some moral antipodes; but it was written for people like ourselves. What we really see at the Globe is mankind weeping. Later we hear of Dr. Johnson weeping. We join a chorus three centuries old in crying out against Cordelia's fate. In doing so we cry out against evil. Why does Croce, the cool and judicious aesthetician, say 'An infinite hatred for deceitful wickedness has inspired this work'? [4] The recoil of our love of Cordelia is a hatred of wickedness. Cordelia we see as its victim.

Shakespearean tragedy does not deal with the punishment of sinners or provide spectacles of personal retribution. It is true enough that wearing the badge of evil confers no immunity. Claudius, Goneril, and the rest must die, and Iago must be hauled off to condign punishment. But Shakespeare goes no further in this direction than he must, and can be as neglectful of the nice distribution of prizes and penalties in tragedy as in comedy. Lucius, Lucullus, Sempronius, and Ventidius, the vile lords of *Timon of Athens*, are simply forgotten, as is the Apothecary of *Romeo and Juliet*. In Broke this character is the scapegoat:

> Th' apothecary, high is hanged by the throte,
> And for the paynes he tooke with him, the
> hangman had his cote.[5]

In Shakespeare there is intimation that Friar Laurence will be forgiven, and, as for the rest, 'Some shall be pardon'd, and some punish'd,' [6] but there are no further particulars. We are not made to think of Romeo, Juliet, and Paris—the flower of Verona—lying dead, and, in atonement, one poor starveling of Mantua swinging on a gibbet. *King Lear* contains a parallel speech:

> All friends shall taste
> The wages of their virtue, and all foes
> The cup of their deservings.[7]

But the prominent 'foes' have all perished by the way; when Edmund, the last of them, is reported dead, Albany says 'That's but a trifle here'; [8] and in the presence of Lear kneeling by the body of Cordelia it is a trifle indeed. The villains are not important enough to be permitted much share in our final emotions. With Macbeth the case is different. His prominence is not intrusive like Iago's: he is the villain and the center of interest, but before he could attain to this position, he had to be a man potentially good. The distinction of Macbeth derives not from the vice in him that meets retribution but from the virtue in him that suffers.

There can be no mistaking about the others. They are not evil ones, but ones in whom evil has found its mark. Shakespearean tragedy is concerned with victims—Romeo, Juliet, Hamlet, Lear, Cordelia, Desdemona, Othello, Timon. One victim may be the agency for transmitting suffering to another—Hamlet to Ophelia, Lear to Cordelia, Othello to Desdemona—but Hamlet, Lear, and Othello remain victims still. Lear in the main is truly more sinned against than sinning, and his suffering is out of all proportion to his offense. The defects of these tragic personages leave in us no residue of satisfaction with their fates. It was Shakespeare's way to dwell upon the suffering of victims and to end his stories with their deaths— the most affecting thing he could do. He exhibits the victory of evil—painful for the bad to be sure, but also painful for the good with whom we are chiefly concerned.

A view such as the above predicates in the plays a clear indication of the nature of the evil which takes its toll. There must be forms of wickedness which are recognizable and avoidable, which can be objectified and hated. The ultimate cause of the suffering must be terrestrial, concrete, human. It cannot be chance. These plays cannot be discussed as 'cosmic' tragedies. It is true enough that tragedy in general affects us in the same part of ourselves as does religion, possibly because religion originates in tragic experience, and a play like *King Lear* leads to religious reflection. But only in those already given to religious doubts would it lead to doubting reflection. Phrases about the play's tearing the universe from its hinges and hurling charges against destiny itself must be viewed as rhetorical flourishes. The enemy in *King Lear* is not God but human unkindness. In *Romeo and Juliet* it is senseless strife, in *Hamlet* earthly venality, in *Macbeth* egotism, in *Othello* envious malice, in *Timon* greed and ingratitude. But these are only words. The enemy is always unkindness behind the familiar visage of one of the seven deadly sins.

The tragedy most often deprecated as a mere display of unfortunate coincidence is *Romeo and Juliet*. It has provoked comment like the following:

When the ending is arbitrary, when instinctively the onlooker feels a desire to intervene and save the hero, as when the voice in the gallery urges Romeo to wait a minute before stabbing himself, for Juliet is but apparently dead—when these sensations spring from the course of a tragedy, the author is failing to convince us that he has grasped the immutable laws of life, it is only intimating to us that he has seen an accident.[9]

This is wittily put, but observe how far the indictment extends: the timely word from the gallery could equally well save Desdemona or Cordelia. Chance operates in all of the plays, comedies as well as tragedies, and part of our interest is in observing its operation. But if it were not for something other than chance, the situation of Romeo would be such that no timely word of warning would be needed. The difference between *Romeo and Juliet* and *King Lear* is only that evil is more formidable in the latter. There is precisely the same display of cause and effect in both plays, and an equal operation of chance, but in *Romeo and Juliet* we feel that there should be more powerful causes for such painful effects. There is too much suffering for too little sin. Yet the play is clear enough about the cause of the disaster. In Bandello from whom, via Boaistuau's *Histoires Tragiques,* all English versions of the story seem to stem, the moral suggested is 'the admonishing of young men, so they should learn to govern themselves with moderation and not rush madly to their own destruction.' [10] Painter omits any explicit statement, but Arthur Broke, who is evidently Shakespeare's immediate authority, does not:

And to this ende (good Reader) is this tragicall matter written to describe unto thee a coople of unfortunate lovers, thralling themselves to unhonest desire, neglecting the authoritie and advise of parents and frendes, conferring their principall counsels with dronken gossyppes, and superstitious friers (the naturally fitte instrumentes of unchastitie) attempting all adventures of peryll, for th attayning of their wicked lust, usyng auricular confession (the kay of whoredome and treason) for furtherance of theyr purpose, abusyng the honorable name of laweful marriage, to cloke the shame of stolne contractes, finallye, by all meanes of unhonest lyfe, hastyng to most unhappye death.[11]

In the body of his poem, Broke contradicts all this by portraying the lovers and even the friar with approval, but the suggestion was there if Shakespeare had cared to follow it. Instead he ignores it and substitutes the following:

The Prologue

Two households, both alike in dignity,
   In fair Verona, where we lay our scene,
From ancient grudge break to new mutiny,
   Where civil blood makes civil hands unclean.
From forth the fatal loins of these two foes
   A pair of star-crossed lovers take their life,
Whose misadventur'd piteous overthrows
   Doth with their death bury their parents' strife.
The fearful passage of their death-mark'd love,
   And the continuance of their parents' rage,
Which, but their children's end, nought could remove,
   Is now the two hours' traffic of our stage . . .

This goes beyond anything in Shakespeare in pointing out the meaning of a play as a whole. Romeo and Juliet are the victims of their 'parents' rage'—are called by Capulet at last 'poor sacrifices to our enmity!' [12] Tybalt is no accident, but the embodiment of the sin of anger. Prince Escalus concludes on a note not found in Broke's poem:

Where be these enemies? Capulet, Montague,
See what a scourge is laid upon your hate,
That heaven finds means to kill your joys with love!
And I, for winking at your discords too,
Have lost a brace of kinsmen. All are punish'd. [13]

We are free to respond in our own way, and even in this unprofound play Shakespeare grants ample scope for individual interpretation, but we cannot say that, by audiences generally, there is nothing to be seen but an 'accident.'

The statements about cosmic questionings in *King Lear* are, although the writers may not recognize the fact, the statements about chance in *Romeo and Juliet*—transposed to a different key. The idea is the same although the vocabulary differs, and although praise is substituted for blame. No lines seem to bite so deep into modern minds as these:

> As flies to wanton boys are we to th' gods.
> They kill us for their sport.[14]

But elsewhere in the play are the lines:

> This shows you are above,
> You justicers, that these our nether crimes
> So speedily can venge! [15]

Neither generalization—no such generalization anywhere in Shakespeare—is presented as final. It is the thought of the speaker in the mood of the moment. In many of the plays besides *King Lear* characters in trouble think of the gods as inimical: the persecuted warrior in *Titus Andronicus,*

> O, why should nature build so foul a den,
> Unless the gods delight in tragedies—[16]

the afflicted maid in *Romeo and Juliet,*

> Alack, alack, that heaven should practice stratagems
> Upon so soft a subject as myself! [17]

the bereaved husband and father in *Macbeth,*

> Did heaven look on
> And would not take their part? [18]

the abused wife in *Cymbeline*,

> . . . if there be
> Yet left in heaven so small a drop of pity
> As a wren's eye, fear'd gods, a part of it!—[19]

the defeated soldier of *Troilus and Cressida*,

> Frown on, you heavens, effect your rage with speed!—[20]

the storm-tossed king of *Pericles*,

> O you gods!
> Why do you make us love your goodly gifts
> And snatch them straight away? We here below
> Recall not what we give, and therein may
> Vie honour with you.[21]

It makes no difference whether the setting is Christian or pagan, or whether the misfortune is real or only apparent. The thought can occur in the most inconsequential comedy; Aegeon says,

> O, had the gods done so [shown pity] I had not now
> Worthily term'd them merciless to us! [22]

It has occurred to no one to find cosmic questionings in *The Comedy of Errors*. The idea that the gods are ill-disposed, that they are well-disposed, that they are indifferent, all find expression in *King Lear*, and in the other plays as well.

The storm is no symbol of merciless fate. It is so viewed by Lear himself, but to adopt his view is to imitate his

frenzy. The idea for the storm comes not from the older
play of *King Leir* but from the subsidiary source in Sidney's *Arcadia*, where the blinded Paphlagonian king is
discovered crouching in a cave for protection from hail
and wintry winds. There, as in Shakespeare's play, the
exposure to the elements is the result of human cruelty.
God made the storm as he made the metal of the weapon
that gouges out Gloucester's eyes. That he made also the
hand that wields the weapon is a legitimate subject for
contemplation but is not forced upon anyone by the play.
The storm is an evil through human intervention. Children
should not drive aged parents into a wet and windy night,
and no one need do so. It is thus that all the characters
except Lear think of it:

> Mine enemy's dog
> Though he had bit me, should have stood that night
> Against my fire.[23]

Not by this play then, nor by any of these seven fables
that end in sorrow, is the spectator robbed of his faith, or,
unless he is predisposed to do so, impelled to think of
himself or mankind as a windlestraw on the flood. The
adversary is not God but earthly sin, the origin of which is
as open a question in Shakespeare as in the world about us.
These plays all treat of *sad particular instances* in which
evil bore its bitter fruit. What can be identified can be
avoided. Plays which make us look at the thing, hate it,
and pity its victims do not offend our sense of justice.

CHAPTER III

JUSTICE IN HISTORY

A concession must be made at once regarding Shakespeare's fourteen history plays. No patriotic Frenchman of
Elizabethan times and no internationalist of our own could
watch the performance of such a play as *King Henry the
Sixth* without having his sense of justice grossly wounded.
The question of partisanship in the histories must be faced
at the outset. Holinshed, in treating the reign of Henry
the Sixth, speaks as follows:

it is a fowle pernicious thing for priuate men, much more noble-
men to be at variance, sith vpon them dependeth manie in affections diverse, whereby factions might grow to the shedding of
bloud . . .[1]

The thought is often expressed by the better characters in
Shakespeare's dramatic treatment of the reign:

> . . . no simple man that sees
> This jarring discord of nobility,
> This shouldering of each other in the court,
> This factious bandying of their favourites,
> But that it doth presage some ill event.[2]

Now Holinshed, although conceding that the English were
unfitted to administer properly their own affairs, assumes
that they have the right to rule the French. He describes
how the 'common and rusticall people in Normandie . . .

expelled certeine English garrisons out of their holds' for 'the black Morian will sooner become white, than the people bred in France will heartilie loue an English borne,' whereupon England's might was turned upon the 'poor catiues' and 'such as were found guiltie were put to terrible executions; as they had well deserved.'[3] He adds, however, with sincere rejoicing, that many were spared. Shakespeare accepts the justice of English severity in France in the manner of his predecessor. This moral naïveté, the expression of mutually contradictory judgments, is familiar to anyone who has read the chronicles and the chronicle plays. In one breath Holinshed can blame both French and English leaders for the wars—'certeine it is, that the onelie and principal cause was, for that the God of peace and loue was not among them'[4]—and in another blame everything upon the failure of the French to yield—'For it standeth not with their envious nature to alter their malicious maners.'[5]

As we read Part One of *King Henry the Sixth*, we find that it is a play about the courage, prowess, and assumed righteousness of the English as represented by such loyal and able leaders as Salisbury, Bedford, Warwick, and, above all, Lord Talbot; and about the opportunism, treachery, and fox-like successes of the French as represented by the fraud and moral depravity of la Pucelle. It shows how France is lost, and Talbot and others martyred to England's internal dissension—Suffolk's ambition, York's rivalry with Somerset, Beaufort's hatred of Humphrey, and so on—in most of which rivalries both sides are in the wrong. The play ends with the punishment of Joan, truce with France, and the ill-omened betrothal of Henry to Margaret. We may compare this panorama with that of *King Henry the Fifth,* in which there is a power strong enough to quell internal dissension, a ruler who is religious, provident, and brave, and who brings happiness and honor to his people and extends the boundaries of his realm—at the expense of the French. What we must realize as we examine such plays is that they are English, and that control of territory across the channel seemed to the English to represent their margin of safety. It is no unfamiliar human phenomenon to see universal moral principles retiring in the face of practical advantages. In Shakespeare's English chronicles, as in Holinshed, these moral principles do not retire from sight but hover, so to speak, in attendance, and when the national interest is not vitally at stake, step forth with all their pristine vigor. In a play like *King Richard the Third,* characters pay moral penalties in every act—Clarence in the first; Edward the Fourth in the second; Grey, Rivers, and Hastings in the third; Queen Anne in the fourth; and Buckingham and Richard in the fifth. Although moral principles are sometimes conscripted in the national cause, and righteousness identified with English aims, this occurs less frequently than in modern propaganda of an analogous sort. Moral principles tend to retain their separate identity in these old chronicles, and there are votes against the English, even when these votes remain uncounted. The naïveté—the very contradictions—is a species of honesty.

The larger question of political partisanship in Shakespeare is a thorny one. That he opposed democracy can be maintained only by identifying democracy with mob-rule. That the plays denounce popular government is an idea that intrenched itself during an era of advocacy of popular government when all that failed to praise it seemed to condemn it. One thing is certain—that the author of these plays would have viewed the contemporary American government with incredulous admiration, a system able to preserve so much order among so much activity and such countless hordes of people. He would, however, since there is a single recognized administrative head, have called our government a monarchy, and would have extended his admiring approval also to the government of communist Russia and of his native land. But these are considerations lying outside the scope of the present volume. At the moment, all we need say is that Shakespeare's plays are not pro-absolutist, pro-aristocratic, or pro-democratic, but are certainly pro-English. Even Victor Hugo is forced to interrupt his ecstasy: Shakespeare 'is very English—too English.' [6] At all other points there is an unsparing treatment of the mixed good and evil on both sides of partisan divisions. This non-partisanship goes beyond anything to be found in Holinshed or Plutarch. The effect sometimes approaches irony; and a populist like Walt Whitman could say, at least on occasion, that Shakespeare's picturing of English kings and English conflicts was intended as an *exposure*.[7] Such is not the case, but often the dramatist's point of view seems to be much like that of Sir Thomas More:

. . . these matters be kings games, as it were stage plaies, and for the more part, plaied vpon scaffolds, in which poore men be but the lookers on. And they that wise be will meddle no further. For they that sometime step vp, and plaie with them, when they can not plaie their parts, they disorder the plaie, and doo themselves no good.[8]

The nationalistic bias which pleased the original audience does not please us, but once we recognize that the chronicles, both English and classical, constitute a distinctive dramatic mode, we must concede that they commit no further offense against a sense of justice.

Something is to be said for that older school of criticism which insisted upon a definition of modes. Although *Coriolanus* is classified as a tragedy in the folio, John Dennis refused to view it as such. He made a proper distinction between a 'Poetical Fiction' and an 'Historical Relation,' and admitted that adherence to the doctrine of poetical justice was an impossibility in the latter. 'The want of this impartial Distribution of Justice makes the *Coriolanus* of Shakespeare to be without Moral,'[9] says Dennis, and he instances the success of murderous Aufidius. Had he pursued the matter a little further, the critic would have perceived that the success and survival of Aufidius in the 'historical relation' invalidates his subsequent declaration that there is want of justice even in the 'poetical fictions.' Nowhere in the latter, the twenty-four fables discussed above, will an Aufidius be found—nowhere a treacherous man who accomplishes his designs against the life of another man and enjoys immunity. If the success of Aufidius is in a separate category, it follows that so also is the failure of Coriolanus—or Brutus, or Hector and Troilus, or Antony and Cleopatra. The fate of these characters is not the fate of Hamlet or Lear or Othello.

It should be apparent to everyone that the endings of Shakespeare's chronicles do not parallel the endings of his tragedies and comedies. They bring no universal joy or sorrow. The failure of Richard is the success of Bolingbroke, the failure of the house of Lancaster is the success of the house of York, the failure of France is the success of England. Agincourt is a comedy for the English but a tragedy for the French. The failure of Troilus and Hector is the success of Diomede and Achilles, the failure of Coriolanus the success of the plebeians and their tribunes, the failure of Brutus the success of Antony and Octavius, the failure of Antony the success of Octavius. Octavius is not an Albany or Fortinbras or Malcolm, ascending an empty throne so that someone may pronounce the obsequies and intimate that life goes on; he is a major character whose will has prevailed and whose cause has won. *King Richard the Third* is considered the nearest approach to formal tragedy among Shakespeare's English chronicles, yet in its implications it is the most joyous because Henry wins Bosworth Field and establishes the house of Tudor. The two parts of *King Henry the Fourth* incorporate a comedy—Shakespeare's eighteenth happy fable at which we laugh and in which we see vice cheated at last of its victory,—but elsewhere in this play chivalrous Hotspur is robbed of his youth, and Hotspur's loss is Prince Hal's gain. There is no moral equity in the contrasted fates of these two young men. *King Henry the Fifth* ends in marriage, but the action of the play is no moral preparative for this marriage in the fashion of comedy. Henry and Katherine are erstwhile opponents only on the basis of nationality; unlike another of Shakespeare's Katherines the lady has not had to be cured of shrewishness, and no impediment has appeared in the character of Henry or those who influence his destiny. Yet *King Henry the Fifth* is more nearly a comedy than *Julius Caesar* is a tragedy.

To what was said earlier about the distinction between the fables and histories something may now be added. The fact that the fable ends in universal joy or sorrow is suggestive: the fable represents elliptically the whole of existence in either of its two aspects; the history, on the other hand, represents—obviously—a segment of existence. The story is not over when the play ends. When *Troilus and Cressida* ends, the Greeks are triumphant, but what of that? When *Coriolanus* opens, the glory that was Greece is scarcely a memory. When *Coriolanus* ends, the popular cause is triumphant, but what of that? When *Julius Caesar* opens a dictator is in power. And thus it goes. There is no mistaking the next sequence. When *Julius Caesar* ends, the triumvirate is in power, but when *Antony and Cleopatra* ends, an emperor stands over the dead body of his last coadjutor. No triumph or defeat has the moral meaning it has in a fable. The empire Octavius ruled was a ruins when Shakespeare wrote, and that fact may explain the somber vein of his Greek and Roman plays: they are not tragedies but segments of a larger tragedy—the fall of an ancient civilization. His English histories, in contrast, may be considered segments of a comedy, and some such conception underlies the common impression that no individual king but England itself is always their hero—England which was riding the crest when Shakespeare wrote.

If this view of the plays seems to attribute to Shakespeare and his original audience more historical sense than we are willing to grant them, it is a fault of the argument as thus far presented. It requires no great historical sense to realize that whatever has happened has happened, and is only a part of a larger whole. An ignorant spectator would have considered Lear and Cornwall just as historical as Coriolanus and Aufidius, but Shakespeare makes sure that he is not penalized by this ignorance. The treatment itself makes clear the distinction. As pointed out earlier, the relationships in the fable are personal and domestic, and the operation of good and evil is not obscured by partisan issues. Lear's enemies, other than his own weakness, are agents of evil; Coriolanus's enemies, other than his own weakness, are rivals in the struggle for power. Aufidius is a bad man, but, unlike Cornwall, he functions in the play as a political opponent rather than as a symbol of evil. The audience could tolerate Aufidius's surviving to speak over the body of Coriolanus, but could not have tolerated Cornwall's surviving to speak over the body of Lear.

The same thing is true of Antony in *Julius Caesar,* not as good a man as Brutus certainly, but a hardy partisan and the avenger of a friend rather than an instrument of evil. There is no Cornwall, or Claudius, or Iago in these chronicles so far as dramatic function as opposed to intrinsic qualities is concerned. Even Joan of Arc, pictured as corrupt and vainglorious, is less Satanic than French; and King Richard the Third is the incarnation of political misrule rather than of moral error, and must perish because he injures England rather than this princeling or that. We may make, nevertheless, an exception of Richard and call him an Iago without injuring our case; in none of the other chronicles is there a character that functions as he does.

We must make a parallel distinction between the heroes of fable and those we are accustomed to see in the role of heroes in the historical plays. We pity Brutus, but he dies as the victim of a political situation, not as the victim of moral evil; in last analysis Brutus is simply a loser. His fate is tragic, but tragic to Brutus rather than to mankind, which is as much as to say that *Julius Caesar* is not a tragedy. Autocracy loses in *Coriolanus* but wins in *Julius Caesar*. To identify autocracy with evil is to call one of these plays a comedy and the other a tragedy. To call them both tragedies is to identify autocracy as a good in one and an evil in the other. To say that the evil in these Greek and Roman plays is national and civil strife is to imply that the English chronicles are also tragedies, for they contain many victims of national and civil strife. To say that the personal defects of the sufferers—in *Antony and Cleopatra* for instance—makes such plays tragedies is to ignore the personal defects of those who are pictured as triumphant, and is to call *King Richard the Second* a tragedy also. As a matter of fact, these chronicles, both English and classical, were called tragedies quite frequently by the Elizabethans themselves. It makes little difference what tag we give them so long as we do not let the tag distort our judgment and obscure the distinctions which must be made. There is no denying that the moral defects of a King Richard the Second and a Mark Antony contribute to the success of a Bolingbroke and an Octavius. We are as much interested in individual characters in the histories as in the fables, often more so, and as much concerned with personal and domestic relationships. But the point is that there are other relationships that make us accept the lack of moral schematization. We sense the fact that the patterns of fable cannot be followed. Dennis was not the last to consider the classical plays as 'historical relations.' Tatlock calls *Troilus and Cressida*, the least historical of them, a 'history,' [10] and Charlton calls it a 'political play.' [11] The rejoinder that its action is more compressed than that of the typical chronicle concerns a point of technique rather than of moral impact, and does not alter the fact that the play deals with predetermined action, with partisan as well as personal morality, and with only a portion of the known lives of its characters. Perhaps Pandar is promising us a *Troilus and Cressida Part Two* in his concluding speech: 'Some two months hence my will shall here be made.' [12] But it does not really matter. There is no final significance in the sorrow of Troilus, or the gaiety of Cressida in the tent of Diomede. The story is not yet over, and the time is yet to come when any Eastcheap drab may be called a 'lazar kite of Cressid's kind.'

It is thus, then, that Shakespeare reckons with the craving for justice in moral mankind. In some of his plays evil misses its mark and is disarmed: the result is happiness. In others evil finds its mark: the result is sorrow. In still others the issue is undetermined: such plays present single acts in the larger drama of history which is always unfolding and in which mingled good and evil bring in their train mingled joy and sorrow. There is justice in all these plays in the largest sense, a satisfying concatenation: unhappiness is never the product of good, and happiness never the product of evil.

Chapter IV

THE SAFE MAJORITY

Twice, characters in Shakespeare fancy themselves in the role of Jehovah about to destroy the Cities of the Plain: Alcibiades as he stands before the 'coward and lascivious town' of Athens,[1] and Coriolanus as he marches upon Rome. To the latter the worthy people of the city seem only 'one poor grain or two' amidst a heap of 'noisome chaff.' [2] Again, in a dialogue between Macduff's wife and little son, it is suggested that the worthy ones of the world are in a minority:

Son. And must they all be hang'd that swear and lie?
Wife. Every one.
Son. Who must hang them?
Wife. Why, the honest men.
Son. Then the liars and swearers are fools; for there are liars and swearers enow to beat the honest men and hang up them.[3]

But there is something wrong with the reckoning; otherwise the relative infrequency of beatings and hangings would establish the dishonest men as very tolerant folk. Shakespeare does not share the view of mankind of Alcibiades, Coriolanus, and little Macduff: the good people in his plays are never a 'saving remnant.'

163

In several of the comedies, *A Midsummer Night's Dream* for instance, not a single human character is seriously defective. In only two of the thirty-eight plays do the defective characters outnumber the rest: *Timon of Athens* and *Troilus and Cressida*. Interestingly enough, these seem to be the only ones which Shakespeare withheld from his general public. In the plays as a whole, the morally sound people compose a comforting majority, and, at least from a statistical angle, the view of human character is optimistic. The analysis which follows has its juvenile features, but it is not irrelevant. The picture presented is the reverse of what would be drawn by a corresponding analysis of the plays of Jonson, Chapman, Marston, or Middleton. Shakespeare stands in this matter, not with the sophisticates, but with Greene, Heywood, Dekker, and those cheerful hacks like Munday, Drayton, Wilson, and Chettle, turning out popular plays in collaborating teams of three, four, and five.

To classify Shakespeare's characters according to moral status requires a suspension of the sense of humor. We must go about this business solemnly, like children at the movies earnestly identifying the 'good guys' and the 'bad guys' so that they may follow their thriller with comfort and understanding. The principles followed in the ensuing classification are as follows. Each character in the plays is considered as the representative of a real human being, and this human being is evaluated as a relative, neighbor, or fellow citizen. His artistic virtues are disregarded. Thus Falstaff is recognized as a delightful fellow but not one we would wish in the guest room as our visiting uncle. All persons in these plays who would embarrass us as relatives or endanger us as neighbors are seriously defective from a moral point of view. Allowances, however, must be made for the milieu in which the character appears. Hotspur in his Shakespearean incarnation would not make a valuable member of a New England town meeting, but Hotspur is faithful to the code of his milieu. Fortunately the distance between neighbors in Hotspur's circle provided considerable elbow room. Some of the characters, even when good-natured, must be classified as bad upon generic grounds: bawds, panders, prostitutes, thieves, and suborned assassins. Some must be considered good on the evidence of a single action or speech: the messenger who conveys his ill-tidings with sympathy, the jailor who offers a word of cheer, the anonymous servant who revolts at cruelty. Such tokens must be allowed to suggest the whole moral pattern of the individual; our theatrical make-up man would have to see to it that his lineaments were benign.

Four categories suggest themselves. First there are those people who are indubitably good: Horatio, Cordelia, Orlando, and Portia the wife of Brutus. This category includes most of the young heroes and heroines of comedy and a host of minor characters whom we evaluate on the strength of a few words and deeds. Second, there are the people good in the main but not proof against temptation or free from flaw: Lear, Friar Laurence, Emilia, Posthumus. Third, there are people bad in the main but with compensating moral qualities or an extenuating background: the Apothecary, King Lewis XI, Cleopatra, Mistress Quickly of Windsor. Fourth, there are the people indubitably bad, either villainous or contemptible: Richard the Third, Iago, Goneril, Joan la Pucelle, Sir Andrew Aguecheek, as well as the troop of petty criminals. We dare not be too subtle. Those slight suggestions of merit and defect which make all the major characters morally stimulating [4] must now be disregarded. Claudius for all his qualms of conscience must be put in category four, and Macbeth along with him. Whatever mixed emotions the character of Macbeth may induce in us, in the practical world we would not wish him as our host. An occasional character must be placed in different categories when he appears in different plays. King Henry the Sixth is saintly at first, but in the last of the trilogy his saintliness is sullied.

Now it can be seen at once that endless disagreements would arise out of the classification thus far suggested. Where shall we put this character or that? To suggest at once the nature of such disagreements, I shall confess that I place Hamlet, Helena, Bottom, and the dramatic Anne Bullen among the indubitably good, but do not place Shylock and Falstaff among the indubitably bad. Shylock is not villainous when thought of at his hearth with Leah and the infant Jessica, nor in the synagogue beside Tubal. These glimpses are not illusions of my mind but are afforded by the play. I am content to call Shylock bad—he vindictively seeks to kill,—but not to group him with Iago. Falstaff, too, though an epitome of vices, has compensating *moral* qualities: he is a cheerful giver of himself and although a buffoon is not contemptible. He is neither slender nor a Master Slender. But these are personal notions only, and it is purely as a matter of curiosity that I submit this first set of figures. In the thirty-eight plays of Shakespeare there are 775 characters of whom we can form a moral estimate. Of these, 378 (49 per cent) are indubitably good, 158 (20 per cent) are good in the main, 106 (14 per cent) are bad in the main, and 133 (17 per cent) are indubitably bad. That only 34 per cent of the total appear as 'mixed' characters is not a defect of the classification; the contrary impression derives from the fact that these mixed characters play the most prominent roles.

The true defect in the figures is that they represent the responses of only one reader and might not even approximate those of another. However, in testing the matter with fellow St. Peters, I discover that differences of opinion nearly always involve the claims of group one as compared with group two, or the claims of group three as compared with group four. My opponent wishes to place Hamlet not in one but in two, and Mistress Overdone in three rather than in four. No one seems to wish to put Hamlet down with the predominately bad, or Macbeth up with the predominately good. When there are only two groupings instead of four, those who pity Shylock most will not place him with Cordelia, and those who admire Isabella least will not place her with Doll Tearsheet or Lady Macbeth. They will twine arms with Falstaff the character but, when it comes to the point, not with the relative or neighbor he represents. The central line of division is distinct enough for statistical purposes, and the following figures have some general validity. Of the 775 characters that can be classified 536 (69 per cent) are on

the side of right, and 239 (31 per cent) on the side of
wrong. Considering that drama is focused on trouble spots,
these figures are cheering. Shakespeare's humanity works
with the angels in the proportion of seven to three. This
is his safe majority.

It is to be expected that in comedy, where virtue prevails in the end, the proportion of good characters will be
greater than in tragedy, where evil prevails in the end.
The percentages are as follows:

	Good Per cent	Bad Per cent
Thirteen comedies [5]	81	19
Four romances	82	18
Seven tragedies [6]	64	36
Ten English chronicles......	63	37
Four classical chronicles	61	39

It is interesting to observe that in this division of characters into sheep and goats, the chronicles follow the pattern of tragedy rather than of comedy, reminding us that
happy is the land that has no history. But even in tragedy
the good characters preponderate. It makes little difference if one follows the traditional classification of the plays
as comedies, tragedies, histories, placing *Julius Caesar,* and
the other Greek or Roman plays with the tragedies. The
proportion of good to bad remains a little better than
eight to two in the comedies, and a little better than six
to four in the tragedies and histories.

The way the women characters divide up is revealing:

	Good Per cent	Bad Per cent
Comedies	96	4
Romances	80	20
Tragedies	42	58
English chronicles	61	39
Classical chronicles	69	31
Women in all the plays......	74	26
Men in all the plays........	68	32

Shakespeare's proportion of good women is greater than his proportion of good men, but not so much greater. In comedy, however, it is conspicuously greater, and a bad woman is a rarity. But in tragedy the bad women outnumber the good, the only category in the plays where the usual proportions are reversed. For Shakespeare it meant woe to the world when the women went wrong.

The most generally reassuring figures are yet to come. They prove that the difference in moral worth of the people in the plays bears no relation to the difference in their social station. An additional word of explanation must precede the table. The characters have been divided into high, middle, and low social classes. The division is only suggestive and corresponds to no hard and fast rule in either our time or Shakespeare's. Knights, lords, and kings are in the high class, but so also are great merchants like Antonio, who if they appeared in the same play with more exalted beings (other than the presiding duke) would have to subside to a humbler place. In other words, the framework of the play determines the classification. English gentlemen are usually placed in the high class, but an indigent younger son like Poins is put in the middle class even though companion to a prince. Falstaff, however, is allowed precedence with his knighthood. The upper household attendants of the high are placed in the middle class, Maria along with Malvolio, though she may be a lady by birth.[7] Captains, friars, doctors, and the like—also teachers—are in the middle class; and artisans, mariners, grooms, common soldiers, citizens of the underworld, and so forth in the low class. It will surprise no one to learn that more than half of Shakespeare's characters, at least of those prominent enough to permit of a moral estimate, are of the high class. The 775 characters divide as follows: high, 465; middle, 156; low, 156. The divisions into moral groupings may be given tabularly:

	Good Per cent	Bad Per cent
Characters of the high class..	69	31
Characters of the middle class	72	28
Characters of the low class...	67	33

The almost equal proportion of good and bad in the three classes is remarkable, especially in view of the fact that so many characters in the low class have been labeled bad on generic grounds as members of the underworld, and also that it has been assumed that suborned assassins ('first murderer' and 'second murderer') belong to the low class. When actually named, like Sir Pierce of Exton in *Richard the Second*, or Sir James Tyrrel in *Richard the Third*, the murderous agent proves sometimes to enjoy considerable social standing. As a matter of fact, the low characters in

Shakespeare nearly always derive their badness from someone higher in the social scale whereas they derive their
goodness from themselves. The high moral rating of
Shakespeare's lower class characters contrasts not only with
the practice of the sophisticated dramatists mentioned
earlier but with that of literary tradition in Shakespeare's
time. Spenser may have been a more advanced social
thinker than Shakespeare; but it is, nevertheless, a rare
forester or fisherman in *The Faerie Queene,* who does not
attempt rape or robbery the moment he comes upon an
unprotected damsel. The *villein* is still the *villain.* Shakespeare seems to have recognized that drama could not
observe the old 'polite' convention and still please the
multitude. On the other hand, the possession of wealth
and power carries with it in his plays no presumption of
moral guilt. His kings and dukes, like his servingmen, are
more often good than bad. Coleridge, offended by that interesting and as yet inadequately studied movement in
which democratic literature was developing its retaliatory
conventions, speaks a truth, although, to the modern reader,
in somewhat mystifying terms:

He [Shakespeare] never inverted the order of nature and pro-
priety, like some modern writers, who suppose every magistrate to
be a glutton or a drunkard, and every poor man humane and
temperate; with him we had no benevolent braziers or sentimental rat catchers.[8]

The statistics in the matter simply confirm what has often
been expressed as a general impression. In the words of
Schelling, Shakespeare deflected 'neither to ridicule nor

respect because of station in life.' [9] This must have meant comfort indeed to a working-class audience. No one in it, however humble, need be disturbed in his inner conviction that on the moral plane—in last analysis the only essential plane—he was any man's equal.

A few more figures may be offered. Shakespeare followed the lead of his sources in respect to the moral composition of his characters, at least to the extent of rarely making good characters bad and bad characters good. When a change is perceptible, it is usually a change for the better. The change is conspicuous enough in cases like Fiorentino's siren of Belmonte's becoming Portia, and Riche's *enceinte* Julina's becoming Olivia, and certainly no pure woman in the sources becomes an impure woman in the plays; but for the most part the gain or loss in moral standing is too difficult to measure to allow of critical agreement or statistical analysis. We are on firmer ground when we study Shakespeare's original creations. Of the 775 characters previously designated, 322 appear in no known source or analogue, or appear only as names. Of these, 72 per cent are good and 28 per cent are bad, thus indicating the dramatist's own preferences and giving us slightly better than our original majority of seven to three—Shakespeare and his audience's safe majority.

The figures simply substantiate what every reader must have learned for himself—that the Shakespearean world is a place to meet fine people and many of them:

> How many goodly creatures are there here!
> How beauteous mankind is! O brave new world
> That has such people in't.[10]

Some rather choice rogues are interspersed in the group of men calling forth this praise from Miranda, but she has the delighted vision of youth and hope—and inexperience. Or perhaps not the latter: some of the rogues have experienced conversion before Miranda sees them—the kind of fifth act conversion ill-naturedly ignored in all the above tabulations. Of course, the cynic may say that Miranda, womanlike, is merely impressed by fine clothes; and none of us can quite forget Prospero's few sad words about Miranda's brave new world: ' 'Tis new to thee.' Still, we may beg the question. We leave the Shakespearean theatre more prone to think of man as a noble piece of work—the 'beauty of the world' [11]—than as a fool on his way to dusty death.

CHAPTER V

THE SENSE OF SOLIDARITY

In *As You Like It*, Orlando stands before Duke Senior begging food and shelter for old Adam and himself:

> If ever you have look'd on better days,
> If ever been where bells have knoll'd to church,
> If ever sat at any good man's feast,
> If ever from your eyelids wip'd a tear
> And knew what 'tis to pity and be pitied,
> Let gentleness my strong enforcement be . . .

The words are echoed by the Duke almost in the fashion of liturgy:

> True is it that we have seen better days,
> And have with holy bell been knoll'd to church,
> And sat at good men's feasts, and wip'd our eyes
> Of drops that sacred pity hath engend'red;
> And therefore sit you down in gentleness,
> And take upon command what help we have.[1]

Personal suffering, religious experience, recollection of kindness in others, sheer instinct,—all go into the making of that quality which Prospero calls the 'virtue of compassion'[2] and smiles at in Miranda. The quality is not confined to the young and maidenly. Pericles stands over the form of Thaisa:

> A terrible childbed hast thou had, my dear;
> No light, no fire. Th' unfriendly elements
> Forget thee utterly.[3]

Except for his thirst after righteousness, tenderness is the most conspicuous quality of Brutus; he will not interrupt the slumbers of his serving boy,[4] and in one scene almost tucks the lad in bed:

> If thou dost nod, thou break'st thy instrument,
> I'll take it from thee; and, good boy, good night.[5]

Troilus and Cressida is a hard play, but the gentleness of the great warrior Hector is remarked upon with peculiar insistence.[6] In *King Henry the Sixth* inhumanity stalks the scene, but not to the exclusion of all else; once, even ferocious Jack Cade, must 'bridle' in himself a feeling of compassion.[7] A touch of feeling in the most ruthless characters of the chronicles prevents them from gloating over fallen foes. The last words are generous and regretful: Charles the Dauphin's [8] upon Lord Talbot, York's [9] upon Clifford, Northumberland's [10] upon York, Bolingbroke's [11] upon Mowbray, Antony's upon Brutus, Octavius's upon Antony, Aufidius's upon Coriolanus, and so on. It is a mere convention, but a gracious one.

It has been remarked of Hamlet's best known soliloquy that the speaker could have had no personal experience of the miseries he enumerates. What does he know of those that 'fardels bear' and 'grunt and sweat under a weary life'? But it is quite common in Shakespeare for personal misery of any kind to be revealed as enlarging the sympathies. Even in ridiculous *Titus Andronicus*, the suffering

175

hero refuses to kill a fly lest he bring upon its relatives sorrows like his own! [12] The most striking example, of course, is provided by *King Lear*. The King's sudden thought of 'poor naked wretches,' his self-objurgation—

> O, I have ta'en
> Too little care of this! Take physic, pomp,
> Expose thyself to feel what wretches feel,
> That thou may'st shake the superflux to them
> And show the heavens more just—[13]

is paralleled in the action by his increasing solicitude for the welfare of his Fool. The charitable thought accompanied by the charitable act is repeated in the career of suffering Gloucester. He gives away his purse, telling heaven to let the man—

> that will not see
> Because he does not feel, feel your pow'rs quickly,
> So distribution should undo excess,
> And each man have enough.[14]

Edgar is the third one in the play to express the idea, describing himself as one—

> Who, by the art of known and feeling sorrows,
> Am pregnant to good pity.[15]

A wonderful thing about this great revelation of the fruits of unkindness is the way it shows kindness being born.

Perhaps it is because compassion grows out of suffering that Shakespeare's poor folk are so compassionate. The scene is constantly illuminated by the kindly and merciful words and deeds of humble and often nameless characters:

Humphrey's servant [16] in *King Henry the Sixth*, Part Two, Rutland's tutor [17] in *King Henry the Sixth*, Part Three, the poor groom [18] in *King Richard the Second*, Corin [19] as well as Adam in *As You Like It*, the sea-captain [20] in *Twelfth Night* (converted from a lustful villain in the source); the servant,[21] in fact most of the servants, in *Julius Caesar*, the steward [22] in *Timon of Athens*, the shepherd and his clownish son [23] in *The Winter's Tale*, the aged tenant [24] in *King Lear*, and that nameless groom who has been Cornwall's servant since childhood, but dies to save Gloucester's eyes. The body of this 'dog' is thrown upon the dunghill.[25] One of the most memorable of these characters is the gardener in *King Richard the Second*. He is sensible and plain-spoken, but kindly above all else, towering in spiritual stature over the queen who has cursed his craft:

> Poor Queen, so that thy state might be no worse,
> I would my skill were subject to thy curse! [26]

Often the note of compassion or mercy is struck by a messenger who has only a single speech in the play. There are those few breathless words of warning to Lady Macduff:

> If you will take a homely man's advice,
> Be not found here. Hence with your little ones! [27]

But all are slain—and another messenger rehearses the tale,

> No mind that's honest
> But in it shares some woe.[28]

The bearers of ill-tidings are always moved by the effect upon the hearer.[29] In some professions hardness of heart is almost a requirement. The duke in *Measure for Measure* says of Claudio's keeper,

> This is a gentle provost. Seldom when
> The steeled jailor is the friend of men.[30]

Shakespeare's jailors, however, are, like this gentle provost, nearly always friends of men.[31] The linking of kindliness and lowliness is so consistent as to amount almost to a law. The lost Imogen exclaims incredulously,

> Two beggars told me
> I could not miss my way. Will poor folks lie
> That have afflictions on them. . . . ? [32]

And we are reminded again of those two proud old men of *Knig Lear* driven into beggary and belated wisdom.

The virtue of compassion in Shakespeare's characters never has an air of display. Any suggestion of sentimentality is eliminated by the spontaneity and brevity of expression. Furthermore, the theme is touched only upon the gravest occasions. There is a little sentimentalizing over the fate of the wounded stag in *Love's Labour's Lost* [33] and *As You Like It*,[34] and the Queen's poisonous experiments upon animals in *Cymbeline* are deplored as callous,[35] but the sufferings of animals are not ordinarily, as in modern literature, equated with the sufferings of men. Launce is fond of his dog, King Richard of his roan Barbary, and carters take care that their 'poor jades' are not 'wrung in the withers,' [36] but that is as far as it goes. There is scant regard shown for the mere sensibilities even of human beings. Hamlet's girding at the old age of Polonius is to modern ears none too pleasant, nor is the reiterated joke about the few drops of blood left in the aged veins of a Nestor,[37] a Menenius,[38] or an Antigonus.[39] Claudio's account of the challenge from Antonio and Leonato in *Much Ado about Nothing*, 'We had lik'd to have had our two noses snapp'd off with two old men without teeth,' [40] is consciously deplorable, but even the approved badinage of the play is blunt enough. Elizabethan manners are not our manners. Imogen and Brutus dog-ear books, and a cold in the head seems a sufficient pretext for Othello to requisition a finely-embroidered handkerchief—a family heirloom and wedding gift to his wife. But Shakespeare's characters are gracious on the whole—much more so than those of any contemporary dramatist. Although Petruchio is rough enough, he declines Kate's challenge to strike her.[41] It would astonish us all if fantastic Petruchio, like Chapman's fantastic Lemot,[42] should lean forward to kiss a woman and should bite her instead!

An interesting chance to compare manners is provided by the three instances in the plays where humble performers try to entertain royalty. In *Love's Labour's Lost*, the Princess of France hears of the village players with glee:

> That sport best pleases that doth least know how;
> Where zeal strives to content, and the contents
> Dies in the zeal of that which it presents.
> Their form confounded makes most form in mirth
> When great things labouring perish in their birth.[43]

She and her companions gibe the performers unmercifully, *humiliating* them, and we must agree for once with Holofernes, 'This is not generous, not gentle, not humble.' [44] In *The Two Noble Kinsmen*, another schoolmaster brings his village troop before royalty, and Theseus and Hippolyta resolve to attend, and do attend, with impeccable politeness. [45] The scene is Fletcher's and somewhat dull. Theseus and Hippolyta behave differently under Shakespeare's management. In *A Midsummer Night's Dream*, Philostrate warns that the play of Bottom and his company—

> . . . is nothing, nothing in the world,
> Unless you can find sport in their intents,
> Extremely stretch'd and conn'd with cruel pain
> To do you service.

Then comes the following dialogue:

> *The.*   I will hear that play;
> For never anything can be amiss
> When simpleness and duty tender it.
> Go bring them in; and take your places, ladies.
>   *Hip.* I love not to see wretchedness o'ercharg'd,
> And duty in his service perishing.
>   *The.* Why, gentle sweet, you shall see no such thing.
>   *Hip.* He says they can do nothing in this kind.
>   *The.* The kinder we, to give them thanks for nothing.
> Our sport shall be to take what they mistake;
> And what poor duty cannot do, noble respect
> Takes it in might, not merit. [46]

This is perfect! And yet this right royal pair refuse to let their kindness spoil their sport—or ours. They, too, gibe the rustic actors. Bottom, however, sagely makes replies; and somehow the one who turns a weaver's beam and the one who wields a scepter are drawn by their maker into a single communion.

Evidently Shakespeare was not too well pleased with his people in *Love's Labour's Lost*. He puts them on a year's probation instead of rewarding them with the usual fifth-act happiness. They have been much given to brittle wit and heartless mockery. Rosaline's remarks to Berowne apply as well to herself and all the company as to him; their 'wounding flouts' and 'gibing spirit' would not have amused the 'speechless sick.' [47] Coleridge is right in saying that only the wicked characters in Shakespeare indulge in habitual scorn.[48] Beatrice is worried when she overhears herself described as a mocker,[49] and there is no character in these plays whom we could pit against Etherege's admired Dorimant and Dorimant's successors. Shakespeare's humor usually follows Rosaline's belated prescription—

> A jest's prosperity lies in the ear
> Of him that hears it, never in the tongue
> Of him that makes it.[50]

The general tendency of Shakespeare's characters, then, is to be compassionate and gracious. At the opposite pole from the compassionate and gracious ones stands the murderer—a figure whose hated role in Shakespeare is the more remarkable in that the plays show little concern for what we have come to call the 'sanctity of life.' The mere killing of a man—by accident or on impulse, as in the case of Hamlet, or in quarrel, as in the case of Romeo—strikes horror into neither the offender nor the onlooker. A good man like Brutus can commit a political assassination and bathe his arms in his victim's blood without feeling any weight of guilt. In the chronicle plays, men kill their enemies with thoughtless dispatch. In the comedies, a character will conceal the true reasons for his exile by saying he has slain a man in fight; [51] it seems a plausible and not too damaging admission. But 'murther most foul'—the premeditated taking of life for malice or personal gain—is something far different. The gentle provost of *Measure for Measure* can pity Claudio but not Barnardine, 'being a murtherer, though he were my brother,' [52] and the good Duke Humphrey of *King Henry the Sixth* makes one exception to his practice of lenience in enforcing the law:

> Murther indeed, that bloody sin, I tortur'd
> Above the felon or what trespass else.[53]

Murder and adultery are, in Shakespeare, the unforgivable sins, and Hamlet believes Claudius, that 'murd'rous, damned Dane,' guilty of both:

> Bloody, bawdy villain!
> Remorseless, treacherous, lecherous, kindless villain! [54]

Not because it is dangerous but because it is *kindless*— unnatural or inhuman—is murder viewed with loathing. The most highly valued quality of kindness, humanity, the 'virtue of compassion,' finds its opposite essence in the spirit of the murderer, who has about him even a distinguishing appearance. Pisanio, when he receives the letter instructing him to slay Imogen, says,

How look I
That I should seem to lack humanity—[55]

and Hubert is accused by King John of having tempted him to plot the death of Arthur simply by being available and by having the look of a murderer.[56] Usually in these plays the hired killers appear in pairs: *Enter two murther-ers.* There are technical reasons for the device, and it is not peculiar to Shakespeare. These subsidiary characters will not be seen again, and it is therefore necessary to suggest at once retribution for an offense so enormous as theirs; one of the pair either demurs at the last moment or expresses immediate remorse: 'O that it were to do!' [52] An interesting exception occurs in *Macbeth.* The pair who murder Banquo upon Macbeth's orders act without compunction before the crime or mutual recrimination after the crime. The reason is obvious. The usual admonitory devices are here unnecessary because we have Macbeth himself and his lady to observe: the whole play is a kind of sequel to that familiar stage-direction, *Enter two murtherers.*

Sigmund Freud has endorsed the view that Macbeth and his lady are a single character split in two: 'she is incarnate remorse after the deed, he incarnate defiance— together they exhaust the possibilities of reaction to the crime . . .' [58] But Macbeth is scarcely 'incarnate defiance.' In Holinshed, he profits in two ways from his later murders: 'they were rid out of his way whome he feared, and then againe his coffers were inriched by their goods . . .' [59]

But, in Shakespeare, Macbeth has no leisure to consider the state of his coffers. He is counting his days and minutes rather than his gold. Yet for neither him nor Lady Macbeth is fear of death the penalty. The penalty is isolation, exclusion from the communion of men, the loss of the sense of solidarity. This is the penalty of the unkind. It is true enough that Macbeth fears retaliation:

> It will have blood, they say; blood will have blood.
> Stones have been known to move and trees to speak,
> Augures and understood relations have
> By maggot-pies and choughs and rooks brought forth
> The secret'st man of blood.[60]

All folklore is in the speech. But the play does not deal so much with the discovery and execution of a murderer as with the loneliness that descends upon him the moment he commits his crime. Both he and his lady begin early to envy their victim, and the final expression of Macbeth's lot comes in the famous lines:

> My way of life
> Is fallen into the sere, the yellow leaf;
> And that which should accompany old age,
> As honour, love, obedience, troops of friends,
> I must not look to have; but, in their stead,
> Curses not loud but deep, mouth-honour, breath,
> Which the poor heart would fain deny, and dare not.[61]

From the moment their crime is committed, neither Macbeth nor Lady Macbeth is granted a single interval of human companionship, warmth, intimacy—even with each other. Macbeth has Seyton to command, but Seyton is remote, unresponsive, humanly a cipher. Macbeth is one of the few characters in Shakespeare penalized by solitude; he alone of the tragic heroes is wholly excluded from the human fold. Hamlet has Horatio, Lear has Kent, Gloucester has Edgar, Coriolanus has Menenius, and the tragic lovers have each other, and loyal friends besides. Brutus can say in almost his last breath,

> My heart doth joy that yet in all my life
> I found no man but he was true to me.[62]

Always in the Shakespearean world, harsh as the fate of man may be, there is someone like Kent, or Emilia, or Beatrice, or Paulina, who, disregarding personal danger and taking the rights of the case on faith, bursts out in angry indignation in defense of the afflicted one. Always there is a wife or parent hovering in the background, interested in one thing only—the personal welfare of their beloved. Volumnia is hard, a Roman mother, but she is counterbalanced by Coriolanus's tender wife. The affairs of a nation mean little more to the Roman wife Portia than to the English wife Lady Percy: they want Brutus and Hotspur to come home safe. Macbeth has no such person, nor has Lady Macbeth: there is nothing in literature to equal the sense of desolation created by the husband's response to news of his lady's death:

> She should have died hereafter—[63]

Timon has Flavius and Hector has Andromache, so that these figures too are linked to the great human fold, but in *Timon of Athens* and *Troilus and Cressida* there is less

sense of solidarity, fewer gracious, loving, and compassionate contacts than in any other of Shakespeare's plays. It is
one of several features that set these two works apart.[64]
The sense of solidarity is strong enough in *Macbeth*; it
enfolds everyone except the murderers.

Unkindness in its most heinous forms—cruelty to blood
kin and ingratitude to benefactors—results in *King Lear*
and *Timon of Athens* in those terrible indictments of mankind voiced by the frenzied victims. The world that Lear
and Timon describe is a putrescent world—the one which
would exist were their cases typical. Sometimes the state of
mankind seems precarious. Gonzalo speaks of Prospero's
spirits—

> Their manners are more gentle, kind, than of
> Our human generation you shall find
> Many—nay, almost any.[65]

But this is not the impression conveyed by the plays as a
whole. Ariel tells Prospero that his affections would become tender if he could now see his suffering enemies.

> *Pros.*　　　　　Dost thou think so, spirit?
> *Ari.*　　　　Mine would, sir, were I human
> *Pros.*　　　　　　　　And mine shall.
> Hast thou which art but air, a touch, a feeling
> Of their afflictions, and shall not myself,
> One of their kind, that relish all as sharply
> Passion as they, be kindlier mov'd than thou art? [66]

Charles Lamb found in William Shakespeare 'a lesson to
teach courtesy, benignity, generosity, humanity' [67]; and
Charles Lamb was a wonderful observer. We are not look-

ing for lessons in the plays, but are thinking of their reassurances. What gives the term 'gentle Shakespeare' its lasting authority and draws concessions of 'endearing qualities' [68] even from Bernard Shaw is the spirit of compassion shown by the characters and for the characters to a degree unequaled elsewhere. This spirit conveys a sense of human solidarity, so that the spectator can experience every emotion except loneliness and despair. We hear, in Elizabethan times, of 'impostumed brains' infecting the theatre, so

> Killing the hearers hearts, that the vast roomes
> Stand empty, like so many Dead-men's toombes.[69]

But these were not Shakespeare's brains. His fellow mortals filled the vast rooms confidently: Shakespeare would not kill their hearts.

Chapter VI

THE ATTAINABLE GOAL

In *The Comedy of Errors* the incipient love affair between Antipholus of Syracuse and Luciana is neglected in the rush of the ending, but no doubt their betrothal will be announced during the 'gossips' feast'[1] to which all the characters repair. They go in 'hand in hand'—the brothers Dromio, the brothers Antipholus, and Aegeon and Aemilia, who have waited thirty-three years for this family reunion. Plautus's *Menaechmi* does not end in this fashion, but in jocular allusions to an auction of the goods (wife included) of one of the twins, valued at something less than fifty thousand sesterces. In *The Two Gentlemen of Verona* the characters go in to 'one feast, one house, one mutual happiness,'[2] and in *The Merry Wives of Windsor* to 'laugh this sport o'er by a country fire, Sir John and all.'[3] The endings are always the same: the feast and dancing, the reunion of kinsmen or restoration of concord among them, the marriage of lovers—Shakespeare's definition of happiness. The things that are valued are brought together gracefully in the fifth act of *The Merchant of Venice*: the beauty of the night, the music, the friendly banter, the moral reflection, the lovers standing side by side. There is, to be sure, restitution of possessions in these endings, the characters get back their titles or their goods;

but that is not where the emphasis falls. *The prize is not prosperity or promotion.*

Even when Shakespeare's worldliest characters are speaking, when hypocrites are paying vice's tribute to virtue, a conspicuous omission usually appears in the list of earthly treasures. Goneril protests that she loves Lear 'No less than life, with grace, health, beauty, honour' [4]; and Ulysses laments that,

> High birth, vigour of bone, desert in service,
> Love, friendship, charity, are subjects all
> To envious and calumniating Time.[5]

There is no mention of riches, power, and getting on in the world. In one of his occasional acidulous moments, Oliver Goldsmith speaks of the characters of fiction being 'lavish enough of their *tin* money,' [6] and, truly enough, Shakespearean characters sometimes show this romantic abandon. Baptista adds thousands of crowns to Kate's dowry when Petruchio proves she is tamed,[7] Portia puts her fortune at Antonio's disposal without reserve,[8] and Celia tosses away her claim to a dukedom with a word, while the reformed Oliver shows equal disregard for inheriting his father's estate.[9] But there is little fanfare about the business. The characters are little interested in acquiring wealth, and little more interested in throwing it away.

Disregard for riches is coupled with nobility in Brutus,[10] Coriolanus,[11] Antony,[12] Duke Orsino,[13] Antonio,[14] France,[15] Hamlet,[16] and many more. The terms of contempt used by Prince Hamlet with respect to that landed gentleman, Osric, 'spacious in the possession of dirt,' [17] are echoed by

Duke Orsino in his dismissal of 'dirty lands,' [18] and by Prince Arviragus in his disgust for those 'who worship dirty gods.' [19] Faulconbridge ends his diatribe against 'commodity' by resolving to seek it himself,[20] but gives no later signs of following the resolution. Bolingbroke wants back his estates but chiefly because they are proof of his gentility.[21] Hotspur will 'cavil on the ninth part of a hair' in a contest of wills, but is ready to sacrifice thrice his gains to 'any well-deserving friend,' [22] and his rival, Hal, shows a kindred spirit:

> I am not covetous for gold,
> Nor care I who doth feed upon my cost;
> It yearns me not if men my garments wear;
> Such outward things dwell not in my desires;
> But if it be a sin to covet honour,
> I am the most offending soul alive.[23]

This is chivalry, and we think of England's 'fiery voluntaries' in *King John*, selling—

> . . . their fortunes at their native homes,
> Bearing their birthrights proudly on their backs
> To make a hazard of new fortunes here.[24]

But freedom from mercenary aims, like other virtues in the plays, is not a matter of social class. Silvia, the duke's daughter of *Two Gentlemen of Verona*, is disdainful of rich Thurio, and Anne Page, the village girl of *Merry Wives of Windsor*, is just as disdainful of rich Slender, her father's choice for her hand:

> O, what a world of vile ill-favour'd faults
> Look handsome in three hundred pounds a year! [25]

In *As You Like It*, the old serving-man gives up his life's savings; and Charles the wrestler, unlike his original in Lodge's *Rosalynde*, is not bribed with money.[26] Williams, the proud private soldier of *King Henry the Fifth*, fails to thank his royal master upon receiving his gloveful of gold and turns angrily upon Fluellen who tries to add a coin to the gift.[27] Even the clowns are magnanimous: Launce claims to want riches,[28] but Launcelot Gobbo prefers the service of poor Bassanio to that of rich Shylock: 'You have the grace of God, sir, and he hath enough.' [29] The servants, almost alone of the characters of *Timon of Athens*, are uncorrupt: Flaminius hurls back the money bribe at Lord Lucullus:

> Fly, damned baseness,
> To him that worships thee. [30]

Although Shakespeare's servants take fees and his clowns sometimes playfully solicit them, there is little true cadging in the plays. 'There's for thy pains,' says music-loving Orsino of *Twelfth Night*. 'No pains, sir. I take pleasure in singing, sir,' [31] replies Feste, yet Feste is the least disinterested of his class.

A few of the gentry show a mercenary taint. Cloten, Thurio, Aguecheek, and one or two others are contemptibly stingy or proud of wealth. Sometimes the mercenary touches are carried over from the sources: Cleopatra holds back some of her treasure,[32] and, in one of the few really ignoble scenes of the chronicles, Buckingham duns Gloucester for the promised 'moveables' of Hereford.[33] In Holinshed, the profit motive is quite conspicuous in the oration to his army made by frugal Henry Tudor; [34] Shakespeare faithfully retains the detail but reduces its expression to a single line.[35] There are fortune-hunters in the comedies as in the body of fiction to which they relate, Petruchio, Fenton, Bassanio, but in some subtle way they have lost their acquisitiveness. Petruchio seems less concerned with money than with conquest, and Bassanio is honest with Portia as well as truly in love.[36] Fenton renounces his original motives entirely.[37] More calculating than any of these is Claudio [38] of *Much Ado about Nothing,* the least amiable lover in Shakespeare. As a class the lovers think of their ladies as France thinks of Cordelia, 'She is herself a dowry.' [39] Any other attitude is treated as comic; Evans sagely remarks that Anne Page's seven hundred pounds and expectations is 'goot gifts,' [40] but Evans scarcely qualifies as a lover.

To say that regard for money is confined to the vicious and contemptible in these plays is true enough but does not give the true picture. Both regard and disregard for money are slighted by the dramatist as themes; money is simply dismissed as uninteresting. At the end of *As You Like It,* the restored duke promises that

> . . . every of this happy number
> That have endur'd shrewd days and nights with us
> Shall share the good of our returned fortunes,
> According to the measure of their states.[41]

In Lodge's *Rosalynde* the individuals are named and awarded specific prizes—high offices and emoluments. There is, in fact, considerable licking of chops. Dramatic economy may be said to have dictated Shakespeare's omissions, but dramatic economy did not dictate the particular class of material he chose to sacrifice. Dowries and settlements are mentioned in the comedies, of course, but without loving detail; figures are given in round numbers or not at all. Usually the financial arrangements are neglected altogether; and the characters never haggle. In Boccaccio's novella of Beltramo and Giglietta, as retold by Painter, the widow names a fee of £100 for her cooperation but is given £500.[42] In *All's Well that Ends Well* there is no bargaining. Helena gives what she has without being asked, and promises an additional thousand crowns.[43] In Twine's *Patterne of Painefull Aduentures,* Tharsia is bid for in specific sums at the slave mart, and the donations made to her later are carefully itemized; [44] indeed for a maiden so virtuous she is surprisingly gainful, more nearly resembling Moll Flanders than the Marina of Shakespeare's *Pericles.*

Crimes against property are seldom treated and never treated in tragic vein; they are not viewed with horror like crimes against life. Shakespeare's swindlers, Falstaff, Sir Toby, Autolycus, are figures of fun. Even that representative of realistic thievery, the waiter in the inn spotting prey for highwaymen,[45] is cheerfully presented; there is some talk of hanging but none of hell-fire. Most wrongs are set right in a fifth act, but no one seems to care if Shallow, or Slender, or Aguecheek, or even the innocent country folk of Bohemia fail to get their money back. Manipulated legacies and marriage settlements, cony-catching, the preying upon citizens' coffers—in general the transfer of money from one pocket to another—is so common a theme in the comedy of Jonson, Middleton, Fletcher, and others as to appear almost a monomania. Shakespeare rarely touches it. Jonson's comedy has been described as an attack upon acquisitiveness, provoked by popular sentiment against the rising tide of capitalism.[46] This is a generous view. Satire has always exploited the opportunity to satisfy an interest in a vice by attacking it; what the concern with money in sophisticated Elizabethan comedy seems truly to reveal is frustration and envy. Shakespeare's comedy gives acquisitiveness the larger reproof of ignoring it. The distinction is not between realistic and romantic subject matter; the emphasis upon the material aspects of the situation is almost as slight in *The Merry Wives of Windsor* as in *Twelfth Night*.

Timon of Athens is the only Shakespearean play in which greed figures as a major motive, and where its ugliness is dwelt upon. 'Ha! what has he sent?' [47] cries Lucullus; and the mistresses of Alcibiades take insults willingly as they stretch forth clutching hands: 'Believe't that we'll do anything for gold.' [48] Normally, Shakespeare avoids the disgusting, and he seems to have found the Lucianic theme of cursed Plutus uncongenial to his talents. There is a greedy old woman in King Henry the Eighth [49]; and elsewhere there are villains like Borachio [50] willing to sell their services for gold, but we look in vain for a full-scale treatment of a miser. Shylock is no miser. However much he resents what Launcelot eats, or shouts about his daughter and his ducats, the ultimate satisfaction he craves is spiritual; we cannot picture him fondling his gold. In *The Taming of the Shrew*, there is a rich old suitor named

Gremio, awaiting development as one of those nasty portraits of cupidity and decay so common in the drama of the age. But Gremio remains a faint forgotten outline, and the play misses utterly the effect usually produced by the type of character and situation.

Shakespeare tells no 'success stories.' The theme that has exercised such terrific compulsion in popular fiction from the time of Daniel Defoe to the time of Horatio Alger, and before and since, is missing from his work. There is a wonderful difference between Prospero's island and Crusoe's. The appeal of Crusoe's is undeniable, but in last analysis it is an appeal of a low order: we are taken to a paradise of possessions, of undisputed ownership, of increasing physical comforts, of success as measured in *things* —satisfactions undiluted by human companionship or competition. Prospero's, in contrast, is the least furnished and most populous 'uninhabited island' imaginable. Good and bad, high and low, drunk and sober trudge up and down its yellow sands. There are nothing but human values in *The Tempest* as in all the plays. That modern malaise expressed in the longing to travel (usually meaning the desire to be with people other than those available), and in the dream of isolation (stone house in the country, or bamboo shack in a South-sea glade), is missing in Shakespeare's characters. They crave neither solitude nor that other modern benison, *security*. Tropical islands and forests of Arden are all very well, but no one wishes to stay with them except the savage and the fantastic. The others prefer the haunts of men. They want life, experience and each other.

There are several long speeches in the plays about the joys of retirement and the pleasures of the simple life—all spoken in self-consolation by those who have had retreat forced upon them: Alexander Iden,[51] Henry the Sixth,[52] Duke Senior,[53] Belarius.[54] All valetudinarians are given their check by the reply of Arviragus to the sermon of Belarius:

> What should we speak of
> When we are old as you? When we shall hear
> The rain and wind beat dark December, how
> In this our pinching cave shall we discourse
> The freezing hours away? We have seen nothing.[55]

There are also long speeches in which the value of life is preached away, by Friar Laurence,[56] Duke Vincentio,[57] Palamon,[58] but always delivered when death seems unavoidable. The melancholy see life as an empty play, and the deeply troubled contemplate suicide. King Henry the Fourth reviews the pangs of existence—

> O, if this were seen,
> The happiest youth, viewing his progress through,
> What perils past, what crosses to ensue,
> Would shut the book and sit him down and die.[59]

But Henry is working out a penance, and for all his laments he clings tenaciously to life. Sentiments like his are always symptomatic of personal distress, and never infect the other characters. Aldous Huxley has recently composed a moral allegory in the guise of a novel,[60] wherein ugly affirmations and allegedly beautiful renunciation struggle for the soul of a *juventus*. A philosophical effusion composed of Indian mysticism with Christian embellishments appears to flow from Shakespeare's lines:

> But thoughts the slaves of life, and life time's fool,
> And time, that takes survey of all the world,
> Must have a stop.[61]

Huxley is shrewd enough to concede that his exegesis is not Shakespeare's, but he might have been more happy in his choice of a spokesman. Huxley's spokesman, of all people to supply texts for renunciators, is Hotspur! But it is Hotspur defeated and dying. The cultist has got his directions crossed, and has mistaken Hotspur's *vale* for an *ave*.

There is no rejection of life in Shakespeare's plays. Death is the great enemy. Everything is excluded that has about it the scent of carrion. Sexual perversion, a common theme today in serious fiction and on the comic stage, is alluded to only once, in *Troilus and Cressida*, and then without curiosity and perhaps even without understanding: 'such preposterous discoveries!' [62] There are no congenital insanity or idiocy, no incest, no mention of abortion, no vicious or depraved children. It is absurd to call Lear's fool an idiot, and the incestuous Antiochus of *Pericles* disappears in a stench before Shakespeare takes up the tale. Children form the single category of Shakespearean characters uniformly untainted. Some of them are pert, and most of them seem to know 'the facts of life,' but they are never guilty or furtive, never evil themselves or the effective instruments of evil. A paternal eye is kept by his creator even upon Falstaff's page, the only brand of the

Boar's Head heap, other than Prince Hal, saved from the burning.[63] In *The Winter's Tale*, Polixenes and Leontes speak fondly of their boyhood when both could have answered the charge of original sin, 'Boldly, "Not Guilty." '

> We knew not
> The doctrine of ill-doing, nor dream'd
> That any did.[64]

Hermione smilingly interprets the avowal to mean that tney 'have tripp'd since,' but the whole exchange is charmingly ideal. All children seem to have come clean into the Shakespearean world.

The parents in the plays are amused by their children and tender toward them. That children may be a trouble or had best be frugally limited in number is a thought that occurs occasionally in other Elizabethan plays but never in Shakespeare's. The artificialities of the sonnets, about the fair and good being obligated to leave the world copies of themselves, are sometimes repeated,[65] but the usual allusion is less precious. The characters seem to desire children simply because children are a good thing to have. The desire crops up in peculiar places: Aaron of *Titus Andronicus* has as his single human quality a love for his child, and Charmian of *Antony and Cleopatra* prays for good fortune —'Let me have a child at fifty . . .' [66] Caesar places Calphurnia where she will be touched to fertility by the runner of the Lupercal.[67] No such episode appears in Plutarch. Shakespeare may be exposing Caesar's superstition, but the more likely explanation is that he observed this Roman couple to be childless and assumed that they regretted the fact. In *The Two Noble Kinsmen* Emily omits from her prayer to Diana one item included by Chaucer's Emelya— 'noght to ben a wyf and be with childe.' [68] Shakespeare's Emily has no aversion to being with child but is simply undecided which of her 'equal precious' suitors should be its father.[69] In *The Winter's Tale*, the ladies remark with delight that Hermione 'rounds apace,' that—

> She is spread of late
> Into a goodly bulk.[70]

More life in the making! There is a kind of innocence to which we have become unaccustomed in Titania's description of the Indian mother:

> . . . we have laugh'd to see the sails conceive
> And grow big-bellied with the wanton wind;
> Which she, with pretty and with swimming gait
> Following (her womb then rich with my young squire)
> Would imitate, and sail upon the land . . .[71]

Mr. Bowdler excluded these lines from his *family* Shakespeare!

That shrewd bit of modern lyricism, 'the rich get richer, and the poor have children,' and that damning indictment of the modern working classes for spending their earnings instead of saving them, suggest something about perennial popular desires and about the vision of happiness in Shakespeare's plays. This vision is certainly improvident, picturing jam today instead of jam tomorrow, and to the fierce thinker may seem hopelessly old-fashioned, socially impractical, and in some respects even disgusting. But the rank and file of most people in most lands in all ages share this vision. Even today, they are sad at the death of a child and joyful at the birth of a child, not having read those books urging that they be sad on both occasions. Shakespeare's spectators are shown a world of folk more highly placed, more handsome, more beautifully attired, less cramped by necessity than themselves. This satisfies their desire for novelty, their curiosity, their exploratory instinct. (The modern motion picture audience is similarly treated.) But among these more brilliant, active, and highly placed people in the plays, the goal is identical with that of the spectators. The goal is the enjoyment of life in the simplest and most available ways. In the Shakespearean world, no one finds happiness in hobbies any more than in wealth, or in climbing or in retreat. There are no stopping places or substitutes. Nothing but living itself will do. The goal, unlike fame or wealth or power or position, is the one thing the spectators as a whole have some hope in achieving. They, too, can sing and dance and talk merrily together, and even look forward to an occasional feast. They can mingle with their kinfolk and love their wives. They can cherish their children. The lords and ladies of the plays can do no more.

The harsh facts of existence bore heavily upon those spectators—more heavily than upon any reader of Shakespeare today. There were thin coats and lean bodies in the throng packed about the scaffold; yet, happiness was imaginable and in a measure attainable. The plays showed its presence and absence in terms which all could understand. London must have been bleak enough outside the Globe in winter twilight, but the wise and indomitable had some kind of hearth to return to, and could, in the spirit of Shakespeare—the exciting, the comforting popular artist— win through to 'one feast, one house, one mutual happiness.'

Notes

PART ONE

CHAPTER I   [PP. 3–15]

MORAL STIMULUS

1. *Winter's Tale*, IV, 4, 118–122.
2. *Ibid.*, IV, 4, 89–90.
3. *Twelfth Night*, II, 3, 36–38.
4. New York, 1924.
5. *Merchant of Venice*, V, 1, 91.
6. *Lear*, III, 4, 82–85.
7. *Othello*, II, 3, 104–107.
8. *Twelfth Night*, V, 1, 47–48.
9. *Julius Caesar*, I, 1, 14–15.
10. *2 Henry Fourth*, II, 2, 104–105.
11. *Romeo and Juliet*, I, 4, 71–88.
12. *Merchant of Venice*, V, 1, 1–22.
13. *Twelfth Night*, II, 4, 30–42, 99–102, 117–121.
14. Boswell, *Life of Johnson*, ed. Hill, II, 98–99.
15. *King Leir*, ed. Hazlitt, *Shakespeare's Library*, Part II, II, 329.
16. *Ibid.*, Part II, II, 374.
17. *Merchant of Venice*, I, 3, 42, 131–138.
18. *Ibid.*, I, 3, 34–40, 49–52; III, 1, 55–76, 126–127; *et passim*.
19. *Ibid.*, IV, 1, 90–100.
20. Stoll, *Shakespeare Studies*, p. 267.
21. *The Orator*, ed. Hazlitt, *Shakespeare's Library*, Part I, I, 356.
22. *King John*, III, 3, 30–55.
23. *Ibid.*, III, 4, 122–169.
24. *Holinshed's Chronicles*, ed. 1807–08, III, 57.
25. *2 Henry IV*, IV, 5, 79.
26. *Holinshed's Chronicles*, ed. 1807–08, III, 65.
27. *Henry V*, II, 4, 102–109; III, 3, 10–41; V, 2, 56–59, *et passim*.
28. *Ibid.*, IV, 6, 35–38; IV, 7, 5–11.
29. *Ibid.*, II, 1, 127–130.
30. *Ibid.*, IV, 7, 42–43.
31. *Titus Andronicus*, II, 4, 22–25.
32. *Ibid.*, I, 1, 391.

CHAPTER II

MORAL RESPONSE

1. Swinburne, *Study of Shakespeare*, p. 227.
2. Schücking, *Character Problems in Shakespeare's Plays*, p. 126.
3. Raleigh, *Shakespeare*, p. 166.
4. Santayana, *Interpretations of Poetry and Religion*, p. 216.
5. Morgann, *On the Dramatic Character of Sir John Falstaff*, p. 286.
6. *Supra*, p. 10.
7. Morgann, *On the Dramatic Character of Sir John Falstaff*, p. 288.
8. Pope, *Preface to The Works of Shakespeare* (1725), p. 169.
9. Theobald, *Preface to The Works of Shakespeare* (1733), p. 190.
10. Warburton, *Preface to The Works of Shakespeare* (1747), p. 241.
11. Smith, *Shakespeare in the Eighteenth Century*, p. 83.
12. Dennis, *Essay on the Genius and Writings of Shakespeare* (1711), p. 9.
13. Stoll, *Shakespeare's Young Lovers*, p. 20.
14. *Romeo and Juliet*, I, 3, 17.
15. *2 Henry VI*, II, 1, 61–134.
16. *Tempest*, II, 2, 145–170.
17. Freud, *Collected Papers*, IV, 321–322; cf. *3 Henry VI*, V, 6, 68–83.
18. Yeats, *Ideas of Good and Evil*, p. 163.
19. Stoll, *Shakespeare Studies*, p. 324.
20. *Ibid.*, p. 327.
21. *Ibid.*, p. 452.
22. *Ibid.*, p. 458.
23. *Coleridge's Shakespearean Criticism*, ed. Raysor, II, 197–198, 229.
24. *Ibid.*, I, 15.
25. Stoll, *Shakespeare Studies*, p. 125.
26. Schücking, *Character Problems in Shakespeare's Plays*, pp. 174 *seq.*
27. *Ibid.*, p. 7.
28. *Ibid.*, p. 235.
29. Stoll, *Shakespeare Studies*, p. 404.
30. *Ibid.*, p. 368.
31. Dowden, *Shakespeare: A Critical Study of His Mind and Art*, p. 377.
32. Pater, "Shakespeare's English Kings," *Appreciations*.
33. Swinburne, *Three Plays of Shakespeare*.

34. Chambers, *Shakespeare: A Survey*, p. 216.
35. Sisson, *Mythical Sorrows of Shakespeare*, p. 58.
36. Stoll, *Shakespeare Studies*, p. 259.
37. Campbell, *Shakespeare's Tragic Heroes*, p. 212.
38. *Hamlet*, I, 2, 11–13.
39. Campbell, *Shakespeare's Tragic Heroes*, p. 141.
40. Lawrence, *Shakespeare's Problem Comedies*, pp. 97–98.
41. Campbell, *Shakespeare's Tragic Heroes*, p. 146.
42. *1 Henry IV*, ed. Kittredge (1940), pp. xii–xiv.

CHAPTER III

HIGHROAD LEADING NOWHERE

1. Johnson, *Preface to the Works of Shakespeare*, p. 262.
2. *Goethe's Literary Essays*, ed. Spingarn, p. 184.
3. Schlegel, *Dramatic Art and Literature*, p. 370.
4. *Coleridge's Shakespearean Criticism*, ed. Raysor, II, 266.
5. Hazlitt, *Characters of Shakespeare's Plays*, p. 347.
6. Birch, *Philosophy and Religion of Shakespeare*, pp. 54–55.
7. Gervinus, *Shakespeare Commentaries*, p. 890.
8. Dowden, *Shakespeare*, p. 34.
9. Croce, *Ariosto, Shakespeare and Corneille*, p. 155.
10. Stoll, *Art and Artifice in Shakespeare*, pp. 165–166.
11. Wilson, "Elizabethan Shakespeare," *Brit. Acad. Lectures*, 1933, pp. 223, 226.
12. Van Doren, *Shakespeare*, p. 6.
13. Shaw, "A Letter from Mr. G. Bernard Shaw," in *Tolstoy on Shakespeare*, p. 168.
14. Ingersoll, *Shakespeare*, Section IV.
15. Herford, *The Normality of Shakespeare's Treatment of Love and Marriage*, p. 4.
16. Craig, *Shakespeare and the Normal World*, p. 4.
17. Johnson, *Preface to Shakespeare*, p. 261.
18. *Goethe's Literary Essays*, ed. Spingarn, p. 184.
19. Schlegel, *Dramatic Art and Literature*, p. 369.
20. *Coleridge's Shakespearean Criticism*, I, 89.
21. Hazlitt, *Characters of Shakespeare's Plays*, pp. 346–347.

22. Dowden, *Shakespeare*, p. 34.
23. Croce, *Ariosto, Shakespeare and Corneille*, pp. 144, 203.
24. Stoll, *Art and Artifice on Shakespeare*, p. 163.
25. Wilson, "Elizabethan Shakespeare," *Brit. Acad. Lectures*, 1933, p. 225.
26. Johnson, *Rasselas*, Chap. X.
27. Johnson, *Preface to Shakespeare*, p. 262.
28. Taine, *History of English Literature*, II, 93.
29. Santayana, *Interpretations of Poetry and Religion*, p. 111.
30. *Ibid.*, p. 117.
31. *Coleridge's Shakespearean Criticism*, II, 141.
32. Hazlitt, *Characters of Shakespeare's Plays*, p. 346.
33. Raleigh, *Shakespeare*, p. 166.
34. Looten, *Shakespeare et la Religion*, 1924.
35. Beeching, *The Character of Shakespeare*, 1917.
36. Cadoux, *Shakespearean Selves*, 1938.
37. Sharp, *Shakespeare's Portrayal of the Moral Life*, 1902.
38. *As You Like It*, II, 3, 44.
39. *Midsummer Night's Dream*, II, 1, 81–117.
40. *2 Henry IV*, Epilogue.
41. *Henry V*, II, Chorus and Scene 2.
42. *1 Henry VI*, II, 5, 84–91.
43. *Antony and Cleopatra*, III, 2, 55–56.
44. *Ibid.*, III, 2, 37–38.
45. *Julius Caesar*, V, 5, 68–75.
46. *As You Like It*, III, 3, 19; cf. also *Twelfth Night*, V, 5, 207.
47. *Troilus and Cressida*, IV, 5, 166–167.
48. *Richard II*, I, 3.
49. Arnold, "The Study of Poetry," *Essays in Criticism*, Second Series, p. 27.
50. Johnson, *Preface to the Works of Shakespeare*, pp. 261–262.
51. Schlegel, *Dramatic Art and Literature*, pp. 369–370.
52. Hazlitt, *Characters of Shakespeare's Plays*, p. 257.
53. Emerson, *Representative Men*, pp. 213–214.
54. Santayana, *Interpretations of Poetry and Religion*, p. 216.
55. *Ibid.*, p. 278.
56. *Tolstoy on Shakespeare*, p. 94.
57. Wright, "Reality and Inconsistency in Shakspere's Characters," *Shaksperian Studies*, 1916, p. 393.

58. Wilson, *Fortunes of Falstaff*, p. 54.
59. Bridges, *The Influence of the Audience*, pp. 12–13.
60. *Ibid.*, pp. 14, 17.
61. Stoll, *Shakespeare's Young Lovers*, pp. 34–35.
62. *2 Henry IV*, Epilogue, 28.
63. *Henry V*, II, Chorus, 40.
64. Horace, *Art of Poetry*, ed. Gilbert, p. 139.
65. *Goethe's Literary Essays*, ed. Spingarn, p. 173.
66. *Lear*, V, 2, 11.
67. *As You Like It*, II, 7, 26–27.
68. Bradley, *Shakesperean Tragedy*, p. 291.

CHAPTER IV

INVOLVEMENT

1. Schlegel, *Dramatic Art and Literature*, p. 370.
2. *Coleridge's Shakespearean Criticism*, ed. Raysor, II, 268.
3. Stoll, *Art and Artifice on Shakespeare*, p. 165.
4. *Macbeth*, IV, 3, 22–24.
5. *Othello*, IV, 3, 107–108.
6. *2 Henry VI*, II, 2, 73–74.
7. *Hamlet*, IV, 7, 136.
8. *Othello*, II, 1, 298.
9. *Julius Caesar*, I, 2, 314.
10. *Cymbeline*, III, 4, 56–58.
11. *Henry V*, II, 2, 93–144.
12. *Troilus and Cressida*, V, 2, 130–136.
13. *Henry V*, IV, 1, 4–5.
14. *Romeo and Juliet*, II, 3, 21–22.
15. *Hamlet*, II, 2, 255–256.
16. *Coriolanus*, IV, 7, 50.
17. *Hamlet*, IV, 7, 118–119.
18. *All's Well*, I, 1, 113–115.
19. *Measure for Measure*, V, 1, 444–446.
20. *All's Well*, IV, 3, 83–84.
21. Wright, "Reality and Inconsistency in Shakspere's Characters," *Shaksperian Studies*, 1916.

22. Morgann, *On the Dramatic Character of Sir John Falstaff*, ed. Smith, pp. 221–222.
23. *Coriolanus*, V, 4, 25–26.
24. Campbell, *Shakespeare's Satire*, pp. 212–213.
25. *Coriolanus*, II, 1, 157–173.
26. *Julius Caesar*, V, 3, 94.
27. Charlton, "Shakespeare. Politics and Politicians," *Eng. Asso. Pamphlet* 72, pp. 20–23.
28. Shaw, "Better than Shakespeare," *Three Plays for Puritans*, p. xxx.
29. *Julius Caesar*, V, 5, 34–35.
30. MacCallum, *Shakespeare's Roman Plays*, pp. 234 *seq.*
31. *Julius Caesar*, V, 1, 30–44.
32. *Timon of Athens*, IV, 3, 300–301.
33. *Ibid.*, I, 2, 108–111.
34. *Ibid.*, IV, 3, 534–536.
35. *Ibid.*, II, 2, 182–183.
36. *Antony and Cleopatra*, I, 4, 27.
37. *Ibid.*, III, 13, 183.
38. *Ibid.*, I, 1, 33–34.
39. *Ibid.*, V, 2, 362–368.
40. *Othello*, I, 1, 66, 88.
41. *Much Ado*, IV, 4, 38; *Troilus and Cressida*, I, 1, 80; *Midsummer Night's Dream*, III, 2, 257.
42. *Titus Andronicus*, IV, 2, 67; see also II, 3, 34; IV, 2, 175.
43. *Merchant of Venice*, II, 1, 1–11.
44. *Ibid.*, I, 2, 143.
45. *Othello*, I, 3, 265–266.
46. *Hamlet*, III, 4, 82–85.
47. *Othello*, I, 3, 293–294.
48. Cinthio, *Hecatommithi*, III, 7, ed. Hazlitt, p. 255.
49. *Othello*, III, 3, 232–233.
50. Sidney, *The Arcadia*, Book II, Chap. 10.
51. *Lear*, IV, 5, 11–13.
52. *Ibid.*, V, 3, 243–244.
53. *Coleridge's Shakespearean Criticism*, ed. Raysor, II, 354.
54. *Lear*, I, 4, 258–273.
55. *Ibid.*, I, 4, 297–311.
56. *Ibid.*, I, 1, 286–312; II, 4, 291–296.

57. *Richard II*, II, 1, 253.
58. *1 Henry IV*, I, 3, 175.
59. *Holinshed's Chronicles*, V, 264, 266.
60. *Ibid.*, V, 270–271.
61. *Macbeth*, V, 8, 4–6.
62. *Holinshed's Chronicles*, III, 57.
63. *1 Henry IV*, I, 1, 24–27; see also *2 Henry IV*, III, 1, 106–108; IV, 4, 1–10.
64. *2 Henry IV*, IV, 5, 210–213.
65. *2 Henry VI*, IV, 2, 130.
66. Chambers, *Shakespeare: A Survey*, p. 319.

CHAPTER V

PARADOXES

1. Bentley, *Shakespeare & Jonson*, I, 120–122.
2. By William Kenrick in 1774. See Smith, *Shakespeare in the Eighteenth Century*, p. 91.
3. Morgann, *On the Dramatic Character of Sir John Falstaff*, 1777.
4. Wilson, *The Fortunes of Falstaff*, 1944.
5. Hugo, *William Shakespeare*, Part II, Book 1, Chap. 2.
6. Taine, *History of English Literature*, II, 93.
7. *Tolstoy on Shakespeare*, p. 70.
8. Stoll, *Shakespeare Studies*, pp. 406–407.
9. Johnson, in 'First Variorum' *Shakespeare*, 1803, XII, 259.
10. *Ibid.*, XII, 505.
11. Raleigh, *Shakespeare and England*, p. 8.
12. *2 Henry IV*, II, 4, 247.
13. *1 Henry IV*, IV, 2, 12–52; V, 4, 166–169.
14. *2 Henry IV*, II, 1, 127.
15. *Ibid.*, II, 4, 283–284.
16. *Ibid.*, II, 4, 418–422.
17. *Ibid.*, V, 3, 140–144.
18. Morgann, *On the Dramatic Character of Sir John Falstaff*, p. 299.
19. Stoll, *Shakespeare Studies*, p. 457.
20. Collier, *A Short View*, 1698, pp. 62, 156.

21. Bridges, *The Influence of the Audience*.
22. *1 Henry IV*, V, 1, 128–140.
23. *2 Henry IV*, IV, 3, 92–135.
24. *Love's Labour's Lost*, I, 1, 72–93, 112–113.
25. *Richard III*, I, 4, 137–148.
26. *All's Well*, I, 3, 45–59.
27. *Ibid.*, I, 1, 134–178; see also *As You Like It*, III, 3, 48–64.
28. *Coriolanus*, IV, 5, 233–250.
29. *Two Gentlemen*, IV, 4, 1–42.
30. *Merry Wives*, III, 5, 97–98.
31. *2 Henry IV*, III, 1, 40–44.
32. *2 Henry IV*, V, 1, 47–51.
33. *Henry V*, II, 3, 20–23.
34. *Tempest*, IV, 1, 209–210.
35. *Romeo and Juliet*, V, 3, 214–242.
36. *2 Henry IV*, II, 4, 85–104.
37. *Merry Wives*, III, 4, 111–113.
38. Santayana, *The Life of Reason: Reason in Art*, p. 171.

CHAPTER VI

ENIGMAS

1. Jonson, *Timber, or Discoveries*, p. 36.
2. *Julius Caesar*, III, 1, 47.
3. *Merchant of Venice*, IV, 1, 216.
4. *All's Well*, III, 7, 46.
5. *Coleridge's Shakespearean Criticism*, ed. Raysor, II, 352.
6. *Antony and Cleopatra*, III, 4, 15–20.
7. *Coriolanus*, V, 3, 106-109.
8. *Julius Caesar*, II, 1, 11–12.
9. *Ibid.*, V, 5, 72.
10. *Two Noble Kinsmen*, I, 2, 98.
11. *Troilus and Cressida*, II, 2, 17, 165–167.
12. *Ibid.*, II, 2, 184–193.
13. *Antony and Cleopatra*, II, 7, 79–86.
14. *King John*, III, 1, 205–206.

15. *Ibid.*, IV, 3, 57–59.
16. *Richard II*, II, 2, 110–115.
17. *1 Henry IV*, IV, 1, 62–65.
18. *2 Henry IV*, Induction, 37.
19. *Ibid.*, II, 3, 47.
20. *Measure for Measure*, V, 1, 38–42.
21. *Ibid.*, V, 1, 442–446.
22. *Ibid.*, I, 3, 35–37.
23. *Hamlet*, III, 2, 381–382.
24. *Ibid.*, IV, 5, 7–10.
25. Saxo Grammaticus, *Historia Danica*, ed. Gollancz, pp. 100, 114.
26. Belleforest, *Histoires Tragiques*, ed. Gollancz, p. 188.
27. *Hamlet*, I, 5, 41–75.
28. *Ibid.*, III, 3, 36–38.
29. *Ibid.*, IV, 5, 17–20.
30. *Ibid.*, II, 2, 57.
31. *Ibid.*, III, 2, 146–157.
32. *Ibid.*, III, 4, 29–30, 53–101.
33. Santayana, *Interpretations of Poetry and Religion*, p. 209.
34. Campbell, *Shakespeare's Tragic Heroes*, p. 128.
35. Santayana, *Interpretations of Poetry and Religion*, pp. 215–216.
36. Belleforest, *Histoires Tragiques*, ed. Gollancz, p. 196.
37. *Hamlet*, I, 5, 189–190.
38. *Ibid.*, II, 2, 593–595.
39. *Ibid.*, III, 1, 84–88.
40. *Ibid.*, IV, 4, 36–46.
41. Furness, *A New Variorum Edition of Shakespeare, Hamlet*, I, iii.
42. *Hamlet*, III, 4, 212.
43. *Ibid.*, IV, 1, 27.

CHAPTER VII

THE UNRELIABLE SPOKESMAN

1. *Richard III*, I, 3, 351.
2. *As You Like It*, V, 4, 109.
3. *Henry V*, II, 4, 74–75.

4. *Othello*, II, 3, 268–269.

5. *Ibid.*, III, 3, 159–161.

6. *Hamlet*, I, 2, 87–106.

7. *All's Well*, I, 1, 64–65.

8. *Hamlet*, I, 3, 55–81.

9. *All's Well*, I, 1, 73–77.

10. Schlegel, *Dramatic Art and Literature*, p. 369.

11. *Measure for Measure*, I, 2, 130–138.

12. *Merchant of Venice*, I, 2, 6–7, 11.

13. *Romeo and Juliet*, III, 3, 108–160.

14. *Comedy of Errors*, II, 1, 34–37.

15. *Richard II*, I, 3, 292–293, 300–303.

16. *Romeo and Juliet*, III, 3, 35, 57–58.

17. *Much Ado*, V, 1, 26–38.

18. *Othello*, I, 3, 218–219.

19. *Two Gentlemen*, II, 7, 75–78.

20. *Merchant of Venice*, I, 1, 87–102.

21. *King Lear*, II, 2, 101–110.

22. *All's Well*, I, 1, 44–52.

23. *Romeo and Juliet*, IV, 5, 66–68.

24. *Julius Caesar*, IV, 3, 23–29.

25. *Ibid.*, IV, 3, 74.

26. *Troilus and Cressida*, III, 3, 145–189.

27. *Taming of the Shrew*, IV, 3, 171–182.

28. *As You Like It*, II, 7, 64–69.

29. *Timon of Athens*, V, 1, 40.

30. *Coleridge's Shakespearean Criticism*, ed. Raysor, I, 111.

31. Campbell, *Shakespeare's Satire*, p. 105.

32. *All's Well*, IV, 3, 1–87.

33. *Coriolanus*, II, 2, 1–40.

34. *Timon of Athens*, III, 2, 71–94.

35. *Richard III*, II, 3, 1–47.

36. *Henry V*, I, 2, 183–212.

37. *Troilus and Cressida*, I, 3, 75–137.

38. *Coriolanus*, I, 1, 99–109, 132–145.

PART TWO

CHAPTER I

JUSTICE IN COMIC FABLE

1. Griffith, *Morality of Shakespeare's Drama*, p. 3.
2. *Ibid.*, p. 15.
3. *Ibid.*, p. 25.
4. *Ibid.*, p. 35.
5. *Ibid.*, p. 51.
6. Rymer, *Tragedies of the Last Age*, p. 23.
7. Addison, *The Spectator*, No. 40.
8. Adler, *Art and Prudence*, p. 67.
9. Bradley, *Shakespearean Tragedy*, pp. 291, 324–326.
10. *Works of Alexander Pope*, eds. Elwin and Courthope, X, 459.
11. Dennis, *On Poetical Justice*, ed. Hooker, p. 20.
12. *Ibid.*, p. 21.
13. Dennis, *On the Genius and Writings of Shakespeare*, ed. Hooker, p. 7.
14. See above, p. 61.
15. *Two Gentlemen of Verona*, V, 4, 55–60.
16. *As You Like It*, II, 3, 17–28.
17. *Winter's Tale*, II, 3, 130–182.
18. *Cymbeline*, III, 2, 1–23.
19. *Tempest*, II, 1, 291–297.
20. *Coleridge's Shakespearean Criticism*, ed. Raysor, I, 113–114.
21. *Ibid.*, II, 352.
22. Pater, "Measure for Measure," *Appreciations*, pp. 189–190.
23. Lawrence, *Shakespeare's Problem Comedies*, p. 117.
24. *Measure for Measure*, V, 1, 405–416, 456–459.
25. Cowan, "Toward an Experimental Definition of Criminal Mind," *Philosophical Essays in Honor of Edgar Arthur Singer, Jr.*, pp. 163–190.
26. *Measure for Measure*, I, 4, 311.
27. *Ibid.*, II, 4, 108.
28. *Ibid.*, II, 2, 89, 139.
29. *Ibid.*, II, 4.

30. Brandes, *William Shakespeare*, p. 620.
31. *Measure for Measure*, II, 1, 17–18.
32. *Hamlet*, II, 2, 554.
33. *Tempest*, V, 1, 292–293.
34. *Much Ado*, V, 4, 1, 129–130.
35. Twine, *Patterne of Painefull Aduentures*, Chap. 23.
36. *Two Gentlemen of Verona*, V, 4, 77–80.
37. *Ibid.*, V, 4, 156–157.
38. *All's Well*, V, 3, 309, 321.
39. *As You Like It*, IV, 3, 136–139.
40. *Ibid.*, V, 4, 165–167.
41. *Tempest*, III, 3, 81–82.
42. *Ibid.*, III, 3, 104–106.
43. *Ibid.*, V, 1, 295.
44. *Measure for Measure*, V, 1, 479–482.
45. *Ibid.*, II, 3, 31–32.
46. Sharp, *Shakespeare's Portrayal of the Moral Life*, p. 147.
47. *Merry Wives*, II, 2, 290–320.
48. *Much Ado about Nothing*, V, 4.
49. *Measure for Measure*, III, 1, 194–199.
50. *Winter's Tale*, I, 2; II, 3.
51. *Comedy of Errors*, IV, 2, 19–22.
52. *Twelfth Night*, III, 4, 401–404.
53. *Midsummer Night's Dream*, V, 1, 410–421.
54. *Titus Andronicus*, III, 1, 205–206.
55. *3 Henry VI*, V, 6, 81–83.
56. *1 Henry IV*, II, 4, 198; *Much Ado*, II, 3, 271; *Macbeth*, IV, 1, 26; *Merchant of Venice*.
57. *Richard III*, I, 4, 228.
58. *2 Henry VI*, II, 1.
59. Stoll, *Shakespeare Studies*, p. 263.
60. *Merchant of Venice*, I, 3, 36–39.
61. *Comedy of Errors*, V, 1, 69–70.
62. *Tempest*, I, 2, 450–452.
63. *As You Like It*, V, 4, 196.

CHAPTER II

JUSTICE IN TRAGIC FABLE

1. *Macbeth*, I, 7, 16–20.
2. *Holinshed's Chronicles*, V, 265.
3. Dennis, *On the Genius and Writings of Shakespeare*, ed. Hooker, p. 7.
4. Croce, *Ariosto, Shakespeare and Corneille*, p. 236.
5. Broke, *Romeus and Iulet*, ed. Hazlitt, p. 203.
6. *Romeo and Juliet*, V, 3, 308.
7. *King Lear*, V, 3, 302–304.
8. *Ibid.*, V, 3, 295.
9. Charlton, "Shakespeare. Politics and Politicians," *Eng. Asso. Pamphlet* 72, p. 6.
10. Bandello, *Novels*, ed. Payne, III, 117.
11. Broke, *Romeus and Iuliet*, ed. Hazlitt, p. 72.
12. *Romeo and Juliet*, V, 3, 304.
13. *Ibid.*, V, 3, 291–295.
14. *King Lear*, IV, 1, 36–37.
15. *Ibid.*, IV, 3, 78–80.
16. *Titus Andronicus*, IV, 1, 59–60.
17. *Romeo and Juliet*, III, 5, 211–212.
18. *Macbeth*, IV, 3, 223–224.
19. *Cymbeline*, IV, 2, 303–305.
20. *Troilus and Cressida*, V, 10, 6.
21. *Pericles*, III, 1, 22–26.
22. *Comedy of Errors*, I, 1, 98–99.
23. *King Lear*, IV, 7, 36–38.

CHAPTER III

JUSTICE IN HISTORY

1. *Holinshed's Chronicles*, III, 154.
2. *1 Henry VI*, IV, 1, 187–191; see also III, 1, 186–200; IV, 3, 47–53.
3. *Holinshed's Chronicles*, III, 179–180.
4. *Ibid.*, III, 183.
5. *Ibid.*, III, 179.

6. Hugo, *William Shakespeare*, Part III, Book 1, Chap. 2.

7. Whitman, "What Lurks Behind Shakespeare's Historical Plays," *November Boughs*, 1888.

8. *Holinshed's Chronicles*, III, 396.

9. Dennis, *Genius and Writings of Shakespeare*, ed. Hooker, p. 6.

10. Tatlock, "The Siege of Troy in Shakespeare and Heywood," *PMLA*, xxx, 769 n.

11. Charlton, "Shakespeare. Politics and Politicians," *Eng. Asso. Pamphlet* 72, p. 19.

12. *Troilus and Cressida*, V, 9, 53.

CHAPTER IV

THE SAFE MAJORITY

1. *Timon of Athens*, V, 4.

2. *Coriolanus*, V, 1, 23–32.

3. *Macbeth*, IV, 2, 51–58.

4. See above, p. 61 *seq.*

5. Including *The Tempest*.

6. Including *Timon of Athens* and *Titus Andronicus*.

7. Draper, "Olivia's Household," *PMLA*, XLIX, 797–806.

8. *Coleridge's Literary Criticism*, ed. Raysor, II, 268.

9. Schelling, "The Common Folk of Shakespeare," *Shakespeare and Demi-science*, p. 99.

10. *The Tempest*, V, 1, 181–184.

11. *Hamlet*, II, 2, 16.

CHAPTER V

THE SENSE OF SOLIDARITY

1. *As You Like It*, II, 7, 113–118, 120–125.

2. *The Tempest*, I, 2, 27.

3. *Pericles*, III, 1, 57–59.

4. *Julius Caesar*, II, 1, 229–230, 252–255.

5. *Ibid.*, IV, 3, 270–272.

6. *Troilus and Cressida*, IV, 5, 106, 182, 189, 227, 257; V, 3, 1, 37, 49; V, 6, 14.

7. *2 Henry VI*, IV, 7, 111–112.
8. *1 Henry VI*, IV, 7, 49–50.
9. *2 Henry VI*, V, 2, 30.
10. *3 Henry VI*, 1, 4, 150, 169–171.
11. *Richard II*, IV, 1, 103–104.
12. *Titus Andronicus*, III, 2, 51–65.
13. *King Lear*, III, 4, 32–36.
14. *Ibid.*, IV, 1, 65–72.
15. *Ibid.*, IV, 6, 226–227.
16. *2 Henry VI*, II, 4, 17.
17. *3 Henry VI*, I, 3, 1–9.
18. *Richard II*, V, 5, 75, 96–97.
19. *As You Like It*, II, 4, 75–79.
20. *Twelfth Night*, I, 2.
21. *Julius Caesar*, III, 1, 280–281.
22. *Timon of Athens*, IV, 3, 502–505.
23. *Winter's Tale*, III, 3, 77, 110, 137–142; IV, 3, 82; V, 2, 164–165.
24. *King Lear*, IV, 1, 13–50.
25. *Ibid.*, III, 7, 95–96.
26. *Richard II*, III, 4, 101–103.
27. *Macbeth*, IV, 2, 68–69.
28. *Ibid.*, IV, 3, 197–199.
29. *Titus Andronicus*, III, 1, 240–241; *2 Henry IV*, I, 1, 65–75; *All's Well*, III, 2, 65–67; etc.
30. *Measure for Measure*, IV, 2, 89–90.
31. *2 Henry VI*, II, 4, 102; *Richard III*, I, 4, 75; *Winter's Tale*, II, 2; etc.
32. *Cymbeline*, III, 5, 8–10.
33. *Love's Labour's Lost*, IV, 1, 31–35.
34. *As You Like It*, II, 1, 21–63.
35. *Cymbeline*, I, 5, 25.
36. *1 Henry IV*, II, 1.
37. *Troilus and Cressida*, I, 3, 291–301.
38. *Coriolanus*, V, 2, 59–62.
39. *Winter's Tale*, II, 3, 165–166.
40. *Much Ado*, V, 1, 115–116.
41. *Taming of the Shrew*, II, 1, 220–223.
42. *An Humorous Day's Mirth*.
43. *Love's Labour's Lost*, V, 2, 517–521.

44. *Ibid.*, V, 2, 632.
45. *Two Noble Kinsmen*, III, 5.
46. *Midsummer's Night's Dream*, V, 1, 78–92.
47. *Love's Labour's Lost*, V, 2, 850–863.
48. *Coleridge's Shakesperean Criticism*, ed. Raysor, I, 135.
49. *Much Ado*, III, 1, 68–70.
50. *Love's Labour's Lost*, V, 2, 870–872.
51. *Taming of the Shrew*, I, 1, 236–237; *Two Gentlemen of Verona*, IV, 1, 26–31.
52. *Measure for Measure*, IV, 2, 65.
53. *2 Henry VI*, III, 1, 131–132.
54. *Hamlet*, II, 2, 607–608.
55. *Cymbeline*, III, 2, 15.
56. *King John*, IV, 2, 216–266.
57. *2 Henry VI*, III, 2, 3; *King John*, IV, 1, 86; *Richard III*, I, 4, 282–284, etc.
58. Freud, *Collected Papers*, ed. Riviere, IV, 332–333.
59. *Holinshed's Chronicles*, V, 274.
60. *Macbeth*, III, 4, 122–126.
61. *Ibid.*, V, 3, 22–28.
62. *Julius Caesar*, V, 5, 34–35.
63. *Macbeth*, V, 5, 17.
64. See above, p. 164.
65. *The Tempest*, III, 3, 32–35.
66. *Ibid.*, V, 1, 18–24.
67. Preface, *Tales from Shakespeare*.
68. Shaw, "A Letter from Mr. G. Bernard Shaw," *Tolstoy on Shakespeare*, p. 168.
69. Dekker, Prologue, *If It Be Not Good the Divel Is In It* (1610–12), 1612.

CHAPTER VI

THE ATTAINABLE GOAL

1. *Comedy of Errors*, V, 1, 405.
2. *Two Gentlemen of Verona*, V, 4, 75.

3. *Merry Wives of Windsor*, V, 5, 256–257.
4. *King Lear*, I, 1, 59.
5. *Troilus and Cressida*, III, 3, 171–174.
6. Goldsmith, *Essay on the Theatre*, 1773.
7. *Taming of the Shrew*, V, 2, 111–115.
8. *Merchant of Venice*, III, 2, 298–308.
9. *As You Like It*, I, 2, 17, 25; V, 2, 6–14.
10. *Julius Caesar*, IV, 3, 26, 74 *et passim*.
11. *Coriolanus*, I, 9, 36–40.
12. *Antony and Cleopatra*, III, 13, 123–125 *et passim*.
13. *Twelfth Night*, II, 4, 84–85.
14. *Merchant of Venice*, I, 1, 155–157.
15. *King Lear*, I, 1, 241–244.
16. *Hamlet*, III, 2, 64–66.
17. *Ibid.*, V, 2, 89–90.
18. *Twelfth Night*, II, 4, 85.
19. *Cymbeline*, III, 6, 56.
20. *King John*, II, 1, 561–598.
21. *Richard II*, III, 1, 26–27.
22. *1 Henry IV*, III, 1, 137–140.
23. *Henry V*, IV, 3, 22–29.
24. *King John*, II, 1, 69–71.
25. *Merry Wives of Windsor*, III, 4, 31–33.
26. *As You Like It*, I, 2, 125–168; Lodge, *Rosalynde*, ed. Hazlitt, p. 24.
27. *Henry V*, IV, 8, 72.
28. *Two Gentlemen of Verona*, III, 1, 361–379.
29. *Merchant of Venice*, II, 2, 159–160.
30. *Timon of Athens*, III, 1, 50–51.
31. *Twelfth Night*, II, 4, 69–70.
32. *Antony and Cleopatra*, V, 2; Plutarch, *Marcus Antonius*, ed. Brooke, p. 130.
33. *Richard III*, IV, 2, 85–124; *Holinshed's Chronicles*, III, 403.
34. *Holinshed's Chronicles*, III, 441–442.
35. *Richard III*, V, 3, 259.
36. *Merchant of Venice*, III, 2, 252–260.
37. *Merry Wives of Windsor*, III, 4, 1–18.
38. *Much Ado about Nothing*, I, 1, 296.
39. *King Lear*, I, 1, 244.

40. *Merry Wives of Windsor*, I, 1, 65.
41. *As You Like It*, V, 4, 178–183.
42. Painter, "Giletta of Norbona," ed. Hazlitt from *Palace of Pleasure*, p. 149.
43. *All's Well*, III, 7, 14, 35.
44. Twine, *Patterne of Painefull Aduentures*, ed. Hazlitt, pp. 296, 298–299.
45. *1 Henry IV*, II, 1.
46. Knights, *Drama & Society in the Age of Jonson*, pp. 200–227.
47. *Timon of Athens*, III, 2, 35.
48. *Ibid.*, IV, 3, 150.
49. *Henry VIII*, II, 3, 23–26, 81–88; V, 1, 171.
50. *Much Ado about Nothing*, III, 3, 121–123.
51. *2 Henry VI*, IV, 10, 18–25.
52. *3 Henry VI*, II, 5, 21–54.
53. *As You Like It*, II, 1, 1–18.
54. *Cymbeline*, III, 3, 10–26, 44–63.
55. *Ibid.*, III, 3, 35–39.
56. *Romeo and Juliet*, IV, 5, 65–83.
57. *Measure for Measure*, III, 1, 5–51.
58. *Two Noble Kinsmen*, V, 4, 1–12.
59. *2 Henry IV*, III, 1, 53–56.
60. Huxley, *Time Must Have a Stop*, pp. 295 *seq.*
61. *1 Henry IV*, V, 4, 81–83.
62. *Troilus and Cressida*, V, 1, 27.
63. *Henry V*, III, 1, 28–58.
64. *Winter's Tale*, I, 2, 69–71.
65. *Romeo and Juliet*, I, 1, 324–327; *Twelfth Night*, I, 5, 259–261.
66. *Antony and Cleopatra*, I, 2, 25–30.
67. *Julius Caesar* I, 2, 6–9.
68. Chaucer, *Knight's Tale*, Globe ed., I, 2306.
69. *Two Noble Kinsmen*, V, 1, 155.
70. *Winter's Tale*, II, 1, 16, 20.
71. *Midsummer Night's Dream*, II, 1, 129–132.

LIST OF WORKS CITED

ADDISON, JOSEPH, The Spectator, No. 40, London, Apr. 16, 1711.

ADLER, MORTIMER, Art and Prudence: A Study in Practical Philosophy. New York, 1937.

ARNOLD, MATTHEW, Essays in Criticism: Second Series (1888). London, 1921.

BANDELLO, MATTEO, Novels (trans. J. Payne). 6 vols. London, 1890.

BEECHING, HENRY C., The Character of Shakespeare (Annual Shakespeare Lecture, British Academy, 1917). London, 1917.

BELLEFOREST, FRANCOIS DE, Histoires Tragiques, Vol. V (1570), ed. Sir Israel Gollancz in The Sources of Hamlet: with Essay on the Legend. London, 1926.

BENTLEY, GERALD E., Shakespeare and Jonson: Their Reputations in the Seventeenth Century Compared. Chicago, 1945.

BIRCH, W. J., An Inquiry into the Philosophy and Religion of Shakspere. London, 1848.

BOSWELL, JAMES, Life of Johnson, ed. George B. Hill. 6 vols. New York, n.d.

BOWDLER, THOMAS, The Family Shakespeare. 6 vols. London, 1860.

BRADLEY, A. C., Shakespearean Tragedy (1904). London, 1915.

BRANDES, GEORGE, William Shakespeare: A Critical Study (1896). New York, 1902.

BRIDGES, ROBERT, The Influence of the Audience (1907). New York, 1926.

BROKE, ARTHUR, The Tragicall Historye of Romeus and Iuliet (1562), ed. W. C. Hazlitt in Shakespeare's Library, Pt. I, Vol. II (London, 1875).

CADOUX, ARTHUR D., Shakespearean Selves: An Essay in Ethics. The Epworth Press, London, 1938.

CAMPBELL, LILY B., Shakespeare's Tragic Heroes: Slaves of Passion. Cambridge, 1930.

CAMPBELL, OSCAR J., Shakespeare's Satire. London and New York, 1943.

CHAMBERS, SIR EDMUND, Shakespeare: A Survey. London, 1925.

CHARLTON, H. B., Shakespeare. Politics and Politicians (English Association Pamphlet No. 72). Oxford, 1929.

CHAUCER, GEOFFREY, Works, ed. Alfred W. Pollard and others (Globe ed.). London, 1925.

CINTHIO (Giovanni Batista Giraldi), Hecatommithi (1565), III, 7, ed. W. C. Hazlitt in Shakespeare's Library, Pt. I, Vol. II (London, 1875).

COLERIDGE, SAMUEL T., Coleridge's Shakesperean Criticism, ed. Thomas M. Raysor. 2 vols. Cambridge, Mass., 1930.

COLLIER, JEREMY, A Short View of the Immorality and Profaneness of the English Stage. 3rd ed., London, 1698.

COWAN, THOMAS, "Toward an Experimental Definition of Criminal Mind," Philosophical Essays in Honor of Edgar Arthur Singer, Jr. Philadelphia, 1942.

CRAIG, HARDIN, Shakespeare and the Normal World (Rice Institute Pamphlet, Vol. XXXI, No. 1). Houston, Texas, 1944.

CROCE, BENEDETTO, Ariosto, Shakespeare, and Corneille, transl. D. Ainslie. London, n.d.

DEKKER, THOMAS, If It Be Not Good the Divel Is in It: A New Play, As It Hath Bin lately Acted, with great applause, by the Queenes Majesties Servants: At the Red Bull. London, 1612.

DENNIS, JOHN, On Poetical Justice (1711), and Essay on the Genius and Writings of Shakespear (1711), both ed. Edward N. Hooker in The Critical Works of John Dennis, Vol. II (Baltimore, 1943).

DOWDEN, EDWARD, Shakspere: A Critical Study of His Mind and Art. London, 1875.

DRAPER, JOHN W., "Olivia's Household," *PMLA*, XLIX, 1934.

EMERSON, R. W., Representative Men. Boston and New York, 1850.

FREUD, SIGMUND, Collected Papers, ed. Joan Riviere. 4 vols. International Psycho-Analytical Press, New York, London, Vienna, 1924.

GERVINUS, G. G., Shakespeare Commentaries (1849–50), transl. F. E. Bunnett. London, 1892.

GOETHE, JOHANN W. VON, Goethe's Literary Essays, ed. J. E. Spingarn. New York, 1921.

GOLDSMITH, OLIVER, "Essay on the Theatre; or, A Comparison Between Sentimental and Laughing Comedy," *Westminster Magazine*, Jan., 1773.

GRIFFITH, ELIZABETH, The Morality of Shakespeare's Drama Illustrated. London, 1775.

HAZLITT, WILLIAM, Characters of Shakespear's Plays (1817), as ed. A. R. Waller and A. Glover in Hazlitt, Collected Works (12 vols., London and New York, 1902–04), Vol. I.

HERFORD, C. H., The Normality of Shakespeare's Treatment of Love and Marriage (English Association Pamphlet No. 47). Oxford, 1920.

HOLINSHED, RAPHAEL, Holinshed's Chronicles of England, Scotland, and Ireland. 6 vols., London, 1807–08.

HORACE, The Art of Poetry, transl. E. H. Blakeney in Literary Criticism, Plato to Dryden, ed. Allan H. Gilbert (New York, 1940).

HUGO, VICTOR, William Shakespeare. Paris, 1864.

HUXLEY, ALDOUS, Time Must Have a Stop. New York, 1944.

JOHNSON, SAMUEL, Preface to the Works of Shakespeare, in 'First Variorum' Shakespeare, ed. Isaac Reed (21 vols., London, 1803), Vol. I.

————Rasselas. London, 1759.

JONSON, BEN, Timber: or, Discoveries: Made upon Men and Matter, ed. M. Castelain. Paris, 1906.

KNIGHTS, L. C., Drama and Society in the Age of Jonson. London, 1937.

LAMB, CHARLES, Preface to Tales from Shakespeare, by Charles and Mary Lamb (2 vols., London, 1807).

LAWRENCE, WILLIAM W., Shakespeare's Problem Comedies. New York, 1931.

LODGE, THOMAS, Rosalynde (1592), ed. W. C. Hazlitt in Shakespeare's Library, Pt. I, Vol. II (London, 1875).

LOOTEN, CAMILLE, Shakespeare et la Religion. Paris, 1924.

MacCALLUM, M. W., Shakespeare's Roman Plays and Their Background. London, 1910.

MOORE, GEORGE, An Anthology of Pure Poetry. New York, 1924.

MORGANN, MAURICE, On the Dramatic Character of Sir John Falstaff (1777), ed. D. N. Smith in Eighteenth Century Essays on Shakespeare (Glasgow, 1903).

PAINTER, WILLIAM, "Giletta of Narbona" (see Boccaccio's Decameron, III, 9), The Palace of Pleasure (1566), ed. W. C. Hazlitt in Shakespeare's Library, Pt. I, Vol. III (London, 1875).

PATER, WALTER, Measure for Measure (1874), and Shakespeare's English Kings (1889), both in Appreciations (New York, 1907).

PLUTARCH, Shakespeare's Plutarch, ed. C. F. Tucker Brooke. 2 vols. New York, 1909.

POPE, ALEXANDER, Preface to the Works of Shakespeare (1725), in 'First Variorum' Shakespeare, ed. Isaac Reed (21 vols., London, 1803), Vol. I.

————Works, ed. W. Elwin and W. J. Courthope. 10 vols. London, 1871–86.

RALEIGH, WALTER, Shakespeare (1907). London, 1928.

————Shakespeare and England (Annual Shakespeare Lecture, British Academy, 1918). London, 1918.

RYMER, THOMAS, The Tragedies of the Last Age. London, 1678.

SANTAYANA, GEORGE, Interpretations of Poetry and Religion (Works, Triton ed., Vol. II). New York, 1936.
———The Life of Reason: Reason in Art. New York, 1905.
———The Middle Span. New York, 1945.
SAXO GRAMMATICUS, Historia Danica, ed. Sir Israel Gollancz in The Sources of Hamlet: with Essay on the Legend (London, 1926).
SCHELLING, FELIX E., "The Common Folk of Shakespeare," in Shakespeare and "Demi-Science." Philadelphia, 1927.
SCHLEGEL, AUGUST W., A Course of Lectures on Dramatic Art and Literature (1809–11), transl. J. Black (Bohn Library). London, 1846.
SCHÜCKING, LEVIN L., Character Problems in Shakespeare's Plays. New York, 1922.
SHAKESPEARE, WILLIAM, Complete Works, ed. George L. Kittredge. Boston, 1936.
———The First Part of King Henry the Fourth, ed. George L. Kittredge. Boston, 1940.
———Hamlet (A New Variorum Edition), ed. Horace H. Furness. 2 vols. Philadelphia, 1877.
SHARP, FRANK C., Shakespeare's Portrayal of the Moral Life. New York, 1902.
SHAW, BERNARD, "Better than Shakespeare," in Three Plays for Puritans (1900). New York, 1931.
———"A Letter from Mr. G. Bernard Shaw," in Tolstoy, Tolstoy on Shakespeare (New York, 1906).
SIDNEY, SIR PHILIP, The Countess of Pembroke's Arcadia (1590), in Complete Works, ed. A. Feuillerat (4 vols., Cambridge, 1912–26).
SILVAYN, ALEX, The Orator, Englished by L. P. (1596), ed. W. C. Hazlitt in Shakespeare's Library, Pt. I, Vol. I (London, 1875).
SISSON, C. J., The Mythical Sorrows of Shakespeare (Annual Shakespeare Lecture, British Academy, 1934). London, 1934.

Smith, David N., Shakespeare in the Eighteenth Century. Oxford, 1928.

Stoll, Elmer E., Art and Artifice in Shakespeare: A Study in Dramatic Contrast and Illusion. Cambridge, 1933.

——Shakespeare Studies, Historical and Comparative in Method. New York, 1927.

——Shakespeare's Young Lovers. Toronto, 1937.

Swinburne, Algernon C., A Study of Shakespeare. London, 1880.

——Three Plays of Shakespeare. New York, 1909.

Taine, H. A., History of English Literature. 4 vols. Philadelphia, n.d.

Tatlock, John P., "The Siege of Troy in Shakespeare and Heywood," *PMLA*, XXX, 1935.

Theobald, Lewis, Preface to the Works of Shakespeare (1733), in 'First Variorum' Shakespeare, ed. Isaac Reed (21 vols., London, 1803), Vol. I.

Tolstoy, Leo, Tolstoy on Shakespeare, transl. V. Tchertkoff and I.F.M. New York, 1906.

True Chronicle History of King Leir, and His Three Daughters, The (c. 1590), ed. W. C. Hazlitt, in Shakespeare's Library, Pt. II, Vol. II (London, 1875).

Twine, Laurence, The Patterne of Painefull Aduentures (c. 1576), ed. W. C. Hazlitt, in Shakespeare's Library, Pt. I, Vol. I (London, 1875).

Van Doren, Mark, Shakespeare. New York, 1939.

Warburton, William, Preface to the Works of Shakespeare (1747), in 'First Variorum' Shakespeare, ed. Isaac Reed (21 vols., London, 1803), Vol. I.

Whitman, Walt, "What Lurks Behind Shakespeare's Historical Plays," in November Boughs (Philadelphia, 1888).

Wilson, John Dover, "The Elizabethan Shakespeare" (in Aspects of Shakespeare, British Academy Lectures by various authors, Oxford, 1933).

——The Fortunes of Falstaff. New York, 1944.

LIST OF WORKS CITED

WRIGHT, ERNEST H., "Reality and Inconsistency in Shakspere's Characters," in Shaksperian Studies by Members of the Department of English and Comparative Literature in Columbia University, ed. B. Matthews and A. H. Thorndike (New York, 1916).

YEATS, WILLIAM B., Ideas of Good and Evil. London, 1903.

INDEX

Pennsylvania Paperbacks

Pennsylvania Paperbacks continued

'Sir, to mine and all mens judgements you seemed dead in this world, wherefore I as your next heire apparent tooke that as mine owne, and not as yours.' Well faire sonne (said the king with a great sigh) what right I had to it, God knoweth. Well (said the prince) if you die king, I will have the garland, and trust to keepe it with the sword against all mine enimies as you have doone. Then said the king, 'I commit all to God, and remember you to doo well.' [24]

In *The Famous Victories of Henry the Fifth*, this matter is reproduced with less rather than more effect, but in Shakespeare's *King Henry the Fourth*, based on both chronicle and older play, every moral as well as emotional stress latent in the situation is injected into the scene—the King's bitter cry in the name of all over-careful fathers 'murd'red' for their pains,[25] the Prince's eager defense, with filial love and self-love intermingled, the sense of guilty past and retributive future, of God and Mammon, of union of human spirits and of their separation. To read the scene and then return to the bald words of the chronicle is to know the richness of Shakespeare's moral assay.

King Henry the Fifth is not considered a play of much subtlety, ethical or otherwise, but it begins to appear so when compared with its cartoon, in this case *The Famous Victories* mentioned above. Shakespeare as usual has deferred to his predecessor's selection of major episodes, but from Holinshed and his imagination he has recruited minor ones. These are of a curious kind. When the Archbishop of Canterbury persuades Henry that he should claim the throne of France, there is no hint of ulterior motive in the older play. The ulterior motive is to be found in Holinshed. The Commons of King Henry has been submitting petitions,

The effect of which supplication was, that the temporall lands devoutlie giuen and disordinatlie spent by religious, and other spirituall persons, should be seized into the kings hands. . . . This bill was much noted, and more feared among the religious sort, whom suerlie it touched verie neere, and therefore to find remedie against it, they determined to assail all waies to put by and over-throw this bill: wherein they thought best to trie if they might mooue the kings mood with some sharpe inuention, that he should not regard the importunate petitions of the commons.[26]

The 'sharpe inuention' was Canterbury's 'pithie oration' upon the *Salique* law, justifying Henry's claim to France. In other words, the idea of conquest was dangled before the King as a diversion. Shakespeare not only admits this matter to his play, but opens the scene with it—a strange way to launch a spectacle of glory. As usual, there is not a trace of commentary, but Henry appears to us as a dupe of Canterbury at least to the extent that Brutus in *Julius Caesar* appears a dupe of Cassius. As the play progresses, the human sufferings accompanying conquest are not dwelt upon, but neither are they, as in *The Famous Victories*, wholly ignored.[27] Having read that Henry 'contrarie to his accustomed gentleness' ordered the slaying of his French prisoners at Agincourt, Shakespeare includes the episode, and although the order is pictured as retaliatory, a shadow has fallen upon the picture.[28] In the famous scene where Henry *incognito* debates with common soldiers a king's responsibility for the death of followers spiritually unprepared, the King is permitted to win, but his conscience is troubled—and so is ours. We should expect a shrewd designer like Shakespeare to let such issues lie dormant if his aim were simply to celebrate a conqueror. Henry's treatment of his old friend Falstaff is not suffered to dwell in oblivion. Early in the play we hear that the old knight's heart is 'fracted and corroborate,' that the 'King hath run bad humours on the knight: that's the even of it';[29] and late in the play blundering Fluellen's comparison of Alexander with his Cleitus and Henry with his Falstaff evokes Gower's troublesome denial: 'Our King is not like him [Alexander] in that. He never kill'd any of his friends.'[30] The interesting thing about all this is that Henry is being presented by Shakespeare as a paragon. In this play alone among his works, we catch, or seem to catch, the note of hero worship; the choruses themselves are a clarion of Henry's glory. But it would seem almost as if the dramatist's artistic habits were exerting pressure of which he was scarcely conscious, and preventing him from doing quite what he intended to do. King Henry is preserved as a paragon of course, but those who dislike this paragon have derived their impressions from Shakespeare, not from *The Famous Victories* or from Holinshed.

It is not merely the exciting quality of Shakespeare's language that transforms his source materials. The changes he makes in the outline, however slight, are crucial. The fact is best illustrated by the play in which he seems to have made no such changes but confined himself to a revision of language, with results that can be described only as disastrous. That *Titus Andronicus* was not Shakespeare's in conception, but pre-existed in 'cartoon' like

13

King Henry the Fifth, is suggested by the presence of episodes habitually eliminated from all other plays of the dramatist, even when they appear in his sources, episodes which might be shown to violate distinguishable Shakespearean *tabus*: a rape attempted and accomplished, an adulterous relationship entered into with thoughtless alacrity, a mother disposed toward infanticide, a father slaying first a son and then a daughter in the interest of some higher ethical 'principle,' a parent encouraging offspring to acts of lust and murder, a victim cruelly maimed with no horrified bystander voicing protests, a subject justifiably slaying his legal emperor, a citizen successfully leading a foreign army against his own nation. The action, conceivably innocuous if baldly presented in the naive manner of *The Famous Victories,* is far from innocuous as garbed in Shakespearean metaphor and moral sentiment. When Lavinia's tongue has been cut out, and her uncle speaks thus—

> Alas, a crimson river of warm blood,
> Like to a bubbling fountain stirr'd with wind,
> Doth rise and fall between thy rosed lips,
> Coming and going with thy honey breath—[31]

we have a typical instance of the rhetorical adornments of the play. The ethical adornments simply blanket it. In the first scene, bloody and barbarous action circles Titus as a hub, and he himself, after making a human sacrifice of a captive enemy, slays his own son and forbids his burial, meanwhile keeping up a steady flow of discourse about virtue, honor, self-sacrifice, and national disinterestedness

Shrewsbury. He lets his son, in fact urges his son, to go to his death against hopeless odds. We never learn why. Worcester says,

> It will be thought
> By some that know not why he is away,
> That wisdom, loyalty, and mere dislike
> Of our proceedings kept the earl from hence.[17]

But what are we to think? The messenger says that North-umberland is sick, then later we are told that he is only 'crafty-sick,' [18] and he makes no defence of his conduct when upbraided by Hotspur's widow. He merely pleads that she cease lamenting 'ancient oversights' [19]—certainly a marvel of understatement. Judging by his conduct, Northumberland is either a traitor, a coward, or a fool; yet he is depicted in the play as none of these things. He remains an enigma.

Consider the case of Angelo in *Measure for Measure*. Which is remarkable—the duplicity of Angelo's character or the duplicity of Shakespeare's play? Considering the mode of presentation, anything we say must be tentative. The character of Angelo is elusive, indeed illusory.

Indictment

Angelo has broken his betrothal to Mariana because she has lost her dowry. To justify his actions to the world, he has cast suspicion upon her chastity. *Angelo is mercenary, a vow-breaker, a hypocrite, cruel, and slanderous.*

Put into supreme authority in Vienna, he enforces a dormant law that makes fornication a capital offense, and condemns Claudio to die. Since Claudio and Julietta are man and wife in all but ceremony, and since their offense was committed while the law was still dormant, they are not true violators. *Angelo is a merciless and unjust judge.*

Claudio's sister, a novice, comes to plead her brother's cause. Angelo proposes to grant a pardon if she will yield her body to him. *Angelo is lustful though a persecutor of lust, and in view of Isabella's consecration to chastity he is perverse.*

She consents, and having enjoyed this enforced assignation, he nevertheless orders the immediate execution of Claudio lest the latter exact vengeance. *Angelo is guilty of rapine, murder, and cowardice*:

> That Angelo's forsworn, is it not strange?
> That Angelo's a murtherer, is't not strange?
> That Angelo is an adulterous thief,
> An hypocrite, a virgin-violator—
> Is it not strange? [20]

The summation is a mild one. In view of the exhaustive list of hideous crimes in this indictment, can any defense exist? Indeed it can.

Defense

The charges above would be valid only if Angelo were a corporeal person whose dreams were realities and whose career was followed chronologically. In the play his initial mistreatment of Mariana is presented to us only after he has become in our eyes a wicked man. It is, so to speak, a projection of his impure present into his pure past. It does not alter the fact that he was in his own eyes and ours a righteous man acting upon principle at the time he condemned Claudio. His proposal to Isabella is the first offense of a chaste man assailed in his weakest spot. Her very purity incites him, because he values purity so much. He would have been proof against the wiles of the most seductive siren. The man was sorely tempted, and he yielded to temptation—nothing more. Furthermore, Isabella was not actually despoiled, and Claudio was not actually executed. The sum of Angelo's guilt is wayward intentions, for which he is publicly humiliated, and which he sincerely repents.

> Look, if it please you, on this man condemn'd
> As if my brother liv'd. I partly think
> A due sincerity governed his deeds
> Till he did look on me. Since it is so,
> Let him not die.[21]

It will be demonstrated later that these lines and their immediate successors plead not mercy but justice—earthly, pragmatic justice—and the play has a logical ending. Angelo's pardon and marriage to Mariana would have been impossible, however, if Shakespeare had abandoned his method of keeping ethical issues suspended. If he had put one canting phrase into Angelo's mouth—as he puts many into Falstaff's,—if he had made Angelo not *precise* but a *precision*, there would have been no enigma. The audience would have recognized a stereotype and prepared to hoot at a Zeal-of-the-Land Busy. As it is, the moral ambiguity of Angelo's role is little greater than that of other principal characters. Duke Vincentio says,

> Sith 'twas my fault to give the people scope,
> 'Twould be my tyranny to strike and gall them
> For what I bid them do.[22]

Is it equitable then, and something other than tyranny, when he places it within the power of a deputy to 'strike and gall them'? It is; but only because, as in the case of Angelo, the consequences of his actions are circumvented. Isabella herself runs a zigzag course in the play. She is at first as anxious to preserve her brother for the uses of this world as to preserve herself for the uses of heaven, then she sacrifices the worldly for the heavenly, and finally the heavenly for the worldly. She was never intended to become a sister of St. Clare in the first place. These are characters in a type of play in which there is cross-cancellation between what happens and what seems to happen. We are amused with phantoms.

The classical instance of the enigma in the plays of Shakespeare is provided by Hamlet. Hamlet's dilemma is so obliquely treated that no two people can see it in precisely the same way, and no agreement will ever be reached on the exact elements of which it is composed. Sometimes our interpretive powers seem challenged directly, as when Hamlet mocks Guildenstern, 'You would play upon me; you would seem to know my stops; you would pluck out the heart of my mystery,'[23] or when immediately after Hamlet's own ambiguities on the value of Fortinbras'